Fishing in Oregon's Best Fly Waters

Scott Richmond

Flying Pencil Publications
Scappoose, Oregon

Published by Flying Pencil Publications in collaboration with Four Rivers Press, Inc.

To receive our catalog of Northwest fishing books, write or call:

Flying Pencil Publications
33126 SW Callahan Road
Scappoose, Oregon 97056
503/543-7171, FAX 503/543-7172

For up-to-the-minute information about fishing in Oregon, visit our Web Site:
www.fishinginoregon.com

Printed in Korea

10 9 8 7 6 5 4 3 2 1

Library of Congress Catalog Card Number: 98-C71182

ISBN: 0-9016473-13-9

Publisher's Notice:

Maps and other information in this book are for planning reference only, not for navigation. Flying Pencil Publications, Four Rivers Press, and the author shall have no liability or responsibility with respect to physical harm, property damage, or any other loss or damage asserted to be caused directly or indirectly by the information in this book.

To Heather and Holly,
who grew up to be adults
I feel privileged to know

Acknowledgments

Randall Kaufmann for fly photos, encouragement, and advice. Maddy Sheehan for maps, editing, and advice. John Laursen for cover design and consultation on book design. Keith Burkhart, Steve and Judy Carothers, Jim Dexter, John Ecklund, Jerry Feliciello, Gavin Grant, Jack Hagan, Bob Jones, Al Kline, Jim Manual, Rich McIntyre, Jeff Perin, Greg Price, Marlon Rampy, Denny Rickards, Dave Roberts, Mike St. John, Scott Wolfe for fishing advice. From the Oregon Department of Fish and Wildlife: Wayne Bowers, Dave Loomis, Steve Marx, Steve Pribyl, Brad Smith, Roger Smith, Amy Stuart, Mark Wade. If I left out anybody who helped, feel free to abuse me for being an absent-minded, ungrateful wretch.

Also by Scott Richmond

The Pocket Gillie
Fishing in Oregon's Deschutes River
Fishing in Oregon's Cascade Lakes
Fishing in Oregon's Endless Season
River Journal: Crane Prairie (forthcoming)
River Journal: Rogue River (forthcoming)

Other Titles from Flying Pencil Publications

Fishing in Oregon
Fishing Washington's Endless Season
Fishing the Oregon Country
Fishing with Small Fry
Steelheading for the Simple Minded

Contents

Maps

LEGEND

Symbol	Description	Symbol	Description
- - - - - - - -	trail or track		boat access
ı ı ı ı ı ı ı ı	railroad	Λ	campground
———	secondary road	◯	county or state road
▬▬▬	major road		U.S. highway
〰	creek		interstate highway
streamflow →	current	☐	forest road
🛆	picnic table		national forest road

How to Use This Book

Fishing in Oregon's Best Fly Waters is divided into three main sections: Trout in Rivers, Trout in Lakes, and Steelhead. These are followed by a collection of useful information, such as hatch charts and fly patterns.

Each of the main sections describes in detail the best fly fishing opportunities, including photos and maps (maps are for planning purposes only, not for navigation). Each section ends with a summary of other opportunities that are pretty good, but not in the same league as those that came before.

Since no two anglers go fishing for identical reasons, "best fly fishing" is subject to personal interpretations. Therefore *Fishing in Oregon's Best Fly Waters* is *my* personal view. I have my prejudices, of course. Given a choice, I usually seek big wild fish swimming in unpolluted rivers and lakes that lie in beautiful settings. I make exceptions, however. For example, Chickahominy Reservoir will never win a beauty contest, and all its trout came from a hatchery. On the other hand, they are big and fat and can be caught in seasons when many other fisheries are less than prime. In any case, I find that most experienced Oregon fly anglers agree with my choices of "best fly waters."

I also think most fly fishers will agree with my selection of fly patterns. They are flies that have proven to be effective in a variety of situations and places. One quick note about the fly patterns: they all assume a Tiemco (TMC) hook; if you use an equivalent style from a different manufacturer, be sure to adjust the hook size since there is no industry standard; a TMC size 12 is *not* the same as a Mustad size 12. The back of the book has recipes for fly patterns not pictured in the other chapters. For anglers with little time or inclination to tie their own flies, the patterns listed here are available in most full-service fly shops.

Fly shops are sources of more than flies and tackle. They can recommend guides, are founts of local wisdom, and can tell you about current conditions. The back of the book has a list of Oregon fly shops.

Besides fly shops and fly patterns, the last chapters include a brief description of hatches and other trout food. That chapter includes a chart listing the most important aquatic insects, the stages that are taken by trout, what fly to use, etc.

While I have tried to make this book as useful as possible to anyone planning to fish in Oregon, *Fishing in Oregon's Best Fly Waters* is not a tutorial for beginning fly anglers. If you are new to the sport, pick up a copy of *The Curtis Creek Manifesto*—a book that has started many fly anglers down the road to success—and my book, *The Pocket Gillie*.

Some other helpful resources are the Oregon Department of Fish and Wildlife (ODFW) fish line; call 800/275-3474 (800-ASK-FISH) to get recorded information on current fishing conditions. Also, my books *Fishing in Oregon's Deschutes River, Fishing in Oregon's Cascade Lakes,* and *Fishing in Oregon's Endless Season* contain a wealth of information on specific fisheries; two other books will be released in 1999 under the *River Journal* series from Frank Amato Publications: one on the Rogue River and the other on Crane Prairie Reservoir. And of course there is the grandaddy of all guide books on Oregon fishing, *Fishing in Oregon,* by Maddy Sheehan and Dan Casali. Anglers with Internet access will find a recent addition to Oregon fishing information at www.fishinginoregon.com.

Releasing Fish

If everyone killed their limit of fish each time they went to a river or lake, the next edition of *Fishing in Oregon's Best Fly Waters* would qualify for "World's Shortest Book." Releasing fish is the best tool we have for preserving quality fisheries. Granted, there are times when a species of gamefish over-populates a river or lake. But not very often. If you want good sport tomorrow, release your fish today.

Just because a fish swims away after it leaves your hand, however, you should not assume it is healthy. A fish that is carelessly handled, then released, may die later the same day, or may be so weakened or injured that it dies a week or month later. It takes care—and caring—to properly catch and release a fish so it stays healthy. Here are a few guidelines.

Use barbless hooks. An easily removed hook reduces the amount of fish handling.

Use the strongest tippet you can get away with. Fragile tippets are not "sporting." They are fish murder. The longer you have to play a fish, the more exhausted it becomes, and the less likely it will recover.

Play fish quickly. If a fish is becoming exhausted from being played too long, clamp the line to the rod and point the rod at the fish. Let it break off.

Watch the water temperature. When the water is above 70 degrees, coldwater fish like trout and steelhead are under stress and should be played quickly. If it's over 75, don't fish.

Don't handle fish when the water warms. Touching a fish with your hands—even if your hands are wet and/or you use a cotton glove—will remove some of the slime coating from the fish. That slime protects the fish against bacteria and disease. When the water is cold, say under 55 degrees, bacteria is not a problem, but when the water warms, it can a life-threatening danger for fish. So when the water temperature is over 55 degrees, play it safe and avoid touching the fish with your hands. If you must touch it briefly, wet your hands first.

Back the hook out carefully. Use a suitable tool such as forceps, pliers, or one of those nifty new catch-and-release tools.

Keep the fish in the water. If you want to take a photo of the fish out of water, get everything set up, then lift the fish and snap the photo quickly. Then immediately put the fish back in the water. Keep the out-of-water time under 15 seconds.

Don't squeeze the fish.

Watch your fingers. Don't put them in the fish's gills or on its eyes. If it isn't a bass, don't hold it by the mouth.

Sacrifice your fly. If the fish is hooked any deeper than the lips, clip off the fly and let it go. Quickly.

Keep it horizontal. Don't grab the fish by the tail, then lift it vertically from the water.

Avoid using a net. Fish get tangled in them and can cause damage to their gills, eyes, and slime coating.

Revive before releasing. To revive a tired fish, grasp it in front of the tail and move it gently back and forth so water works through its gills. Don't let go the first time the fish tries to swim away; let go the second time.

Block the current. In a river, block the current with your upstream leg and revive your fish in the quiet water behind it.

Watch for signs of exhaustion. If a fish rolls over on its side or back, it's exhausted. Take special care of it.

Don't dump a fish into fast water. It can start to tumble and not be able to get in a position so it can breath.

Trout in Rivers

Lower Deschutes River

A robust population of hard-fighting, wild native rainbow trout. Spectacular basalt walls that tower a thousand feet over white-water rapids. A ribbon of life through a desert eco-system. How do I even begin to describe this river, the most famous of Oregon's fly waters?

The delight of finessing a fussy trout lying near shore under an arch of alder branches. The rush that comes when an aggressive rainbow smacks a fly and runs the reel into its backing in a few heartbeats. The satisfaction of tightening the line on a fish that just intercepted a drifting nymph. Can mere words convey the emotions of fishing the Deschutes?

Nope. You'll just have to come and experience it yourself.

I have more than a few friends who wish I wouldn't encourage anglers to come to the Deschutes, but they'll have to put up with me. I think everyone should fish here at some time in their life. As more people appreciate and, above all, *understand* this river, the more likely it will be well cared for. The rivers that are in the most trouble are the ones with the fewest friends.

Not that the Deschutes lacks admirers. It is Oregon's premier fly fishery. A blue-ribbon stream for both trout and summer steelhead, it has the advantage (and disadvantage) of being close enough for the majority of the state's anglers to make a day trip.

Most of the river is now open year-round, and fishing can be excellent any month of the year. It can also be poor, because this is a moody river in any season. Also, because the Deschutes supports a rich diversity of aquatic insects, trout have a lot of food to choose from—and anglers can have a tough time figuring out what fly to tie on. The river has its delights, but it also has its frustrations.

Anglers are not the only visitors here.

The lower 100 miles of the Deschutes flow through a magnificent basalt canyon over 1,000 feet deep.

The Deschutes is extremely popular with whitewater enthusiasts, and rafters and kayakers outnumber anglers in some seasons and on some stretches. Heavy use has resulted in heavy regulation; you might feel you need an extra tackle bag just to carry around permits: fishing license, boaters pass, steelhead tag (if steelheading), tribal license (if fishing on the Warm Springs Reservation). Those drifting the river have additional restrictions on when and where they can float the Deschutes.

Some anglers complain that the river is too crowded and, worst of all, "it's not like it used to be." Well, yes. There are more people flogging the water with fly rods than there were 15 years ago. As the years glide by, both anglers and curmudgeons increase in num-

ber. But it's still a pretty good river. And if you are clever about when you come and where you go, you can find a lot of untouched water.

As for "river managers" and "cognizant government agencies," they are an unfortunate consequence of more people using the river. While a few rules and limitations may be annoying, they're better than having hoards of people and no rules.

Managed, mis-managed, beloved, heavily used, and too frequently abused, the Deschutes keeps flowing through its awe-inspiring canyon. Somehow trout thrive, and anglers are still graced with moments of sublime pleasure.

Access and Facilities

Warm Springs. The boat ramp is a quarter mile south of the Hwy. 26 bridge over the Deschutes (near mile post 105). There is some bank access near the ramp, and a bit more farther south along Hwy. 26; look for turnouts. Day-use only.

Mecca Flat. From the east end of the Hwy. 26 bridge, turn north onto a dirt road. Take the third left and follow it 1.5 miles to Mecca Flat; the road is sometimes rough. There is camping at Mecca Flat. Trails follow the riverbank 7.5 miles to Trout Creek Campground, and fishing can be excellent all the way. The upper trail is an old railroad bed and is suitable for mountain bikes.

Dry Creek. Near the town of Warm Springs, turn off Hwy. 26 onto Warm Springs Route 3. Go north 3.1 miles, then turn right onto a gravel road where you see a sign for Dry Creek. Take the right fork when the road splits. The campground is about two miles farther. If you have a tribal permit, you can fish six miles of river between Dry Creek and Trout Creek. There is a good trail all the way. Mountain bikes may be used.

Trout Creek. From the community of Gateway, take Trout Creek Road about four miles to the river. Trails lead upstream to Mecca Flat (7.5 miles), and bank access is excellent. Mountain bikes are permitted. There is no downstream access.

South Junction. Turn onto a gravel road near the junction of Highways 97 and 197. South Junction is nine miles down this road. There are 1.5 miles of public water here, and a campground.

Maupin. Hwy. 197 crosses the Deschutes at Maupin. Access roads follow the river bank upstream for six miles, and downstream about 30 miles to Macks Canyon. Nearly all of this is public land. There are numerous campgrounds and boat ramps along the way (see the maps), as well as bank access. Above Maupin, there is bank access beyond the locked gate (six miles from town). Beyond this gate you may walk the road all the way to North Junction, but you may not drive it or use a bicycle. Below Macks Canyon, it is possible to walk the old railroad bed, but it's a tough slog for the first four miles.

Oak Springs. From Hwy. 197 north of Maupin, turn down a gravel road where you see a sign for the ODFW hatchery. The river is about three miles distant. Park near the railroad tracks. There are no facilities.

Kloan. From The Dalles, go through the communities of Petersburg and Fairbanks. About 12.5 miles from The Dalles, turn onto Fulton Rd. After 1.6 miles, take the right fork and travel a narrow, very rough and dangerously steep gravel road (impassable in wet weather) to Kloan. There is bank access at Kloan, but no facilities and no boat launching.

Heritage Landing. This boat ramp is at the river's mouth on the west side. Trails lead upstream, offering good bank access.

Deschutes River State Park. At the mouth of the river on the east bank. Camping is excellent, with the usual RV-oriented facilities. Near the park entrance there is an old road that leads upriver all the the way to Macks Canyon. You can walk or use a mountain bike; no cars, however.

When to Fish

Below the Warm Springs Reservation boundary (river mile 67), the Deschutes is open all year. December and January are lean months for trout fishing, but the Deschutes fishes well from February through November. Above the reservation boundary, fishing opens the fourth Saturday in April.

Kaufmann's Stone
(Randall Kaufmann)

Hook:	5263, sizes 2-6
Thread:	Black
Antennae:	Black turkey biot
Tail:	Same as antennae
Rib:	Amber Swannundaze
Abdomen:	Make a blend of angora goat in various colors to look iridescent; use black purple, claret, red, amber, brown, blue, and orange. Mix 2:1 with black Haretron
Wingcases:	Three sections of turkey quill. Coat with Flexament and clip to shape before tying
Legs:	Round black rubber
Thorax:	Same as abdomen
Head:	Same as abdomen

Vary colors to match species. Most of the big *Pteronarcys* (salmonfly) nymphs are black, with some chocolate brown ones. The slightly smaller golden stoneflies are more of a mottled tan; use size 8-12 hooks for them.

This fly must be fished on the bottom. Period. So weight it heavily with lead wire under the body; wrap the lead, then flatten it with pliers. For extra weight, put on a bead head. Yes, you're going to lose a lot of flies.

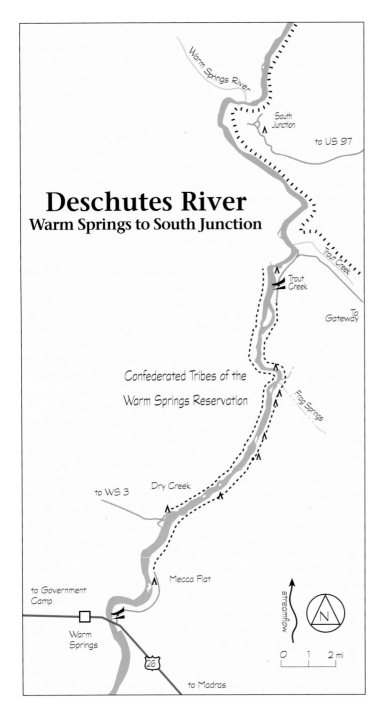

Deschutes River
Warm Springs to South Junction

Species

All trout are wild native rainbows of a desert-adapted strain known as "redsides" (which is not the same as "redband"). The river also holds countless numbers of mountain whitefish, as well as steelhead. An occasional bull trout shows up, especially near Pelton Dam.

Services

Maupin has tourist-oriented services, as does Madras and The Dalles. Warm Springs does not. There are a few services in Biggs, near the river's mouth.

Deschutes Canyon Fly Shop in Maupin is a good source of supplies, and there are fly shops in Bend, Sunriver, and Sisters. Anglers headed here from Portland can make a stop at the Fly Fishing Shop in Welches, on Hwy. 26 between Sandy and Government Camp.

Hatches and Other Food

This is a rich river. Pick up a rock, and you will find it crawling with insects. The profusion and diversity of food often makes it difficult to determine just what the trout want. Always carry some kind of seine so you can examine what bugs are in the water. Even then you will have evenings when five species of insects are floating by, and the trout could be taking any of three stages of each species.

Here are the most common insects you will encounter.

Giant Stonefly/Salmonfly. Trout eat stonefly nymphs all year, but especially April through early June and again in fall. Salmonflies—the adult version—begin hatching in mid-May near Maupin, with the hatch working its way upstream to Warm Springs in a week or two.

Golden Stonefly. These nymphs are also quite common and are taken most of the year. The hatch begins about two weeks after the onset of the salmonflies. When adults of both species are present, trout usually prefer golden stones.

Caddis. The Deschutes is a caddis-rich river. Green rock worms, spotted caddis, saddle-case caddis, weedy-water caddis, and October caddis are all present. The numbers of the first two species diminish as the river warms below Maupin.

Green rock worms have two hatch periods: May, and September-October. Spotted caddis larvae are prominent in the upper stretch of the river, and trout take them nearly all year.

Pale Morning Dun. This mayfly dominates the river from late June through mid-July. Dry flies work well when cast in quiet runs, under overhanging alders, and near shore.

Blue-Winged Olive. From October through April, this diminutive mayfly rules the river. Hatches occur most afternoons, with backeddies and slow runs the best places. The best hatches are on drizzly days.

Mahogany Dun. September often finds these mayflies hatching in slow water near shore. Fishing can be excellent but difficult.

Midges. Midges are a common evening hatch. Backeddies, current seams, and slow runs are the best places to cast a pupa pattern that matches the size and color of the natural. Use a seine to figure out what's in the drift. This can be a frustrating hatch because there are so many naturals that you don't know if trout are ignoring you because you have the wrong pattern, a bad drift, too thick a leader, or just because your fly was one among a million and they couldn't sip everything that floated by.

Other hatches. There are sporadic and occasionally important hatches of yellow quills, green drakes, and March browns.

Fishing Tips

Divide the River. It's a big, imposing river, and no one can cast to all of it. So divide it in thirds and treat the part closest to you like it is the *only* river. Read it for current seams, backeddies, breaks, riffles, etc., and forget all that water you can't reach.

Prime places. The prime places to fish are: backeddies; deeper water just below a riffle; near the bank just downstream from overhanging alder branches; boulder fields; drop-offs; current seams; runs of moderate current and medium depth.

It's never all good. At any time on any day, only one or two of the prime places listed above will have good fishing. If you don't know what's happening, fish each type of water until you find which ones are productive. Then look for other places that are just like that, and ignore the rest.

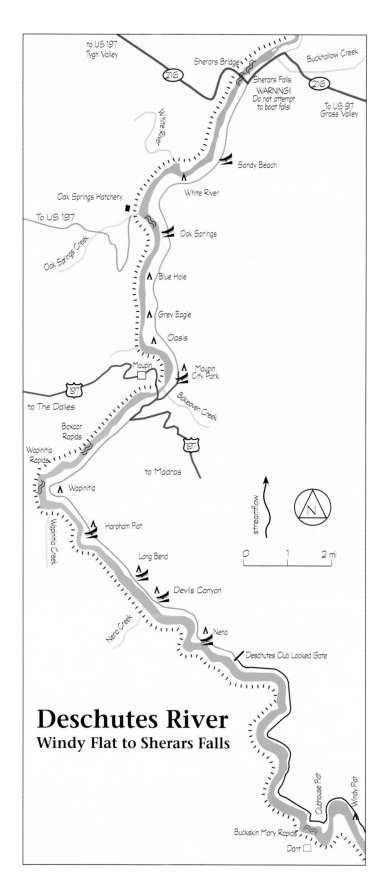

Deschutes River
Windy Flat to Sherars Falls

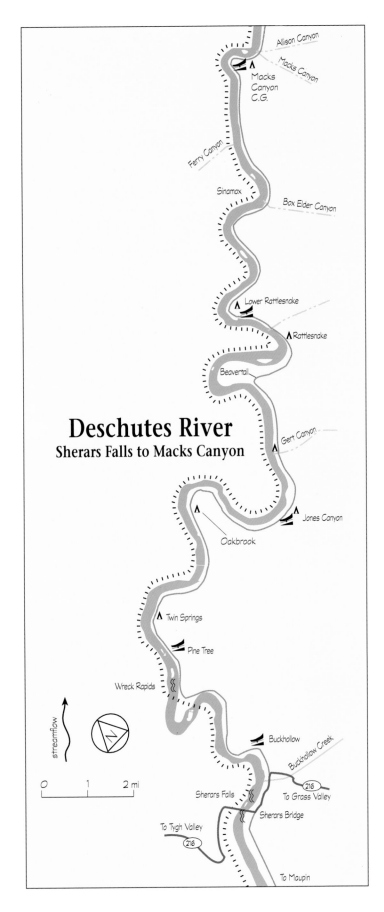

Deschutes River
Sherars Falls to Macks Canyon

Two-nymph rigs work well. You can fish two nymphs at once by tying a large one to the end of the leader, then tying 18 inches of leader to the hook bend with a clinch knot; tie a smaller nymph to the end of this short leader. Or, cut the leader about a foot from the end, then re-connect it with a blood knot, leaving a six-inch tag out the middle of the knot; tie a small nymph on the tag end, and a large nymph on the leader end.

Where your fly should be. With rare exceptions, your fly should be on the surface, within six inches of the surface, or within six inches of the bottom. You won't catch many fish between these places except sometimes with a fly that is moving from the bottom to the surface.

Pick your dry fly by water type. Dry flies should have the least amount of hackle necessary to float the fly. In rough, riffly water you need a high floating fly with lots of hackle. In slower water, your fly needs much less hackle. Most of my Deschutes dry flies have the hackle trimmed off the bottom so the fly will ride lower in the water.

Dealing with refusals. Sometimes a trout rises to your fly and doesn't take it. Usually this means the trout got close to the fly, then veered off at the last minute because it didn't look right. Either your fly is not right (usually it's too big, sometimes it's the wrong color or pattern) or your tippet is too thick. Change to a smaller fly. If that doesn't work, try changing patterns, then color. If you still are refused, go to a smaller diameter tippet.

Backeddies. In a backeddy, the current forms a "lazy susan" that traps drifting food and delivers it to trout. The best place for a trout to be is at the head of the backeddy, where the circling, upstream current meets the main downstream current. The next best place is the outside seam. Both are devilishly difficult to fish because the contrary currents prevent a drag-free drift. To combat this, use a long, thin tippet that will wiggle in the current. Then cast it so you get some loose line and leader that the current can pull out, giving your fly a few more moments of drag-free drift.

Every backeddy is different, and it takes patience to learn each one: where to stand, where to cast, how to get the right drift. Watch the foam; usually there will be occasional surges of current that will push foam in front. Trout will be in the leading edge of this "push," so cast to it and hope for the best. And sometimes there is just no way you are going to get a good enough drift to catch a decent fish. Recognize when you're beaten, and move on to more productive water.

Leaders. Except in winter, this is not a clear river. A nine-foot leader tapered to 5X works fine when fishing dry flies or just subsurface. Sometimes a 6X leader will help in backeddies. When fishing stonefly nymphs, use a 2X or 3X tippet.

Slow down. Most anglers walk too fast or drift by quickly in a boat. If they don't see a rise in two seconds they keep walking or drifting until they spot one. Slow down! Most of the time you'll only see an occasional rise in a backeddy or along a grassy bank, or the subtle subsurface flash of a trout feeding on nymphs. Study each likely place. If it's good water it will have trout in it, and if you take your time you'll soon see where they are.

Be stealthy. Move slowly near fish; don't wade if you don't have to; keep a low profile; don't splash around; and don't cast until you have a good idea where the fish are.

Take care with spawners. When you see lots of large, dark-hued fish in shallow water in April and May, they're spawning trout. Leave them alone and fish elsewhere.

Take care with smolts. In May, there are hoards of seven-inch steelhead and salmon smolts, especially in the backeddies. They're idiots for anything resembling live food, so don't throw them a fly, dry or otherwise. You want to catch them two years later when they come back as mature, sassy steelhead that will make your reel smoke.

Special Regulations

Artificial flies and lures only. No angling from a floating device. No wild (not fin-clipped) steelhead may be kept. Maximum

Stimulator
(Randall Kaufmann)

Hook:	200R, sizes 6-10
Thread:	Fire orange
Tail:	Golden-brown elk
Rib:	Copper or gold wire
Abdomen:	Blend of gold, ginger, amber, yellow goat with golden-brown Haretron. Palmer with blue dun hackle
Wing:	Golden-brown elk
Hackle:	Furnace
Thorax:	Fire orange Antron

The Stimulator is a versatile pattern. This recipe will imitate an adult golden stonefly, but tied on a smaller hook and with a lighter wing and a yellow body, it will represent a little yellow stonefly. On a size 4 hook with an orange body, it resembles the salmonfly. I use an orange version on a size 8 hook to imitate an October caddis. The fly floats well in rough water, but on calmer drifts I trim the hackle on the underside so it will float a little lower.

bag limit of two trout per day; 10 inch minimum, 13 inch maximum. Boaters Pass required to float any portion. A special permit is required to fish the Warm Springs Reservation section.

Note: See pages 90-91 for additional Deschutes maps.

Metolius River

The Metolius is a river of jaw-dropping beauty and hard-to-catch trout. It rises from vast underground reservoirs near the volcanic cone of Black Butte. Additional springs swell the flow, and it soon becomes a broad, swift-flowing river, one of the three big streams that join to form the lower Deschutes.

The Cascade crest is only a few miles west—close enough that the Metolius has a forested setting, but far enough that the big

Pacific storms stop about five or ten miles away. So the days are usually sunny, if not warm, and the nights are cool. The mature ponderosa pines that surround the river give it a park-like appearance. I doubt you'll find a more beautiful place to fish in Oregon, or maybe anywhere else.

A few years ago, hatchery stocking ceased, and the river is now managed for wild native rainbow trout. The typical fish is 13-15 inches long, but there are trout that top five pounds. Above Bridge 99, the regulations call for fly-fishing-only, catch-and-release. Below Bridge 99, artificial lures are permitted, but no bait. The river is not suited to boating.

Being spring-fed, the Metolius runs cold (mid-forties), clear, and constant. So when other rivers are high and muddy, the Metolius is still fishable. It is one of the most reliable destinations for winter fly anglers. It is also one of the toughest rivers in the state to fish well. The clarity of the water, the twisting, difficult currents, and the diversity of the hatches make for difficult fishing. But if the fish seem reluctant, let your senses revel in the gorgeous surroundings.

Wild trout swimming in a crystalline river that flows through a beautiful forest—if you don't enjoy fly fishing here, you have no soul.

Access and Facilities

Turn off Hwy. 20 onto FR 14 (west of Sisters and Black Butte, east of Suttle Lake), then follow signs for Camp Sherman. FR 14 gives paved access to the east bank as far as Bridge 99. A jolting dirt road (FR 1499) continues downriver. FR 1420-400 takes you to a nice campsite, as does FR 1270-980. Rough trails follow the river almost everywhere.

Near Camp Sherman, most of the west side is private property. Below Candle Creek the west bank is within the Warm Springs Reservation and has no public access.

There are many campgrounds along the river, especially near Camp Sherman. The Riverside walk-in sites are particularly pleasant places for tent campers. You can camp below Bridge 99 on the east side, but there are no facilities (and no fees).

The road below Bridge 99 is currently scheduled to be closed to automobiles sometime in the future.

When to Fish

The Metolius is fishable and accessible all year, although December through March your wader boots will be crunching snow.

Species

Since 1997, the Metolius has been managed for wild, native trout. No more fish will be stocked in the river. Most of the fish are rainbows, but there are still a few browns and brook trout. The average rainbow is 13-15 inches long, with enough fish over five pounds to keep you on your toes.

The Metolius is fast and cold. There just

Green Drake Paradrake
(Carl Richards and Doug Swisher)

Hook:	900BL, size 8-12
Thread:	Olive
Wing:	Black or dark gray elk hair. Wing should appear wide from side, narrow from front.
Tail:	Moose
Body:	Olive elk hair. Tie in front of wing with hairs facing forward, and wrap up to hook eye. Then pull hair back along hook shank to make an extended body. Wrap with thread from head to tail.
Hackle:	Olive-dyed grizzly tied parachute style

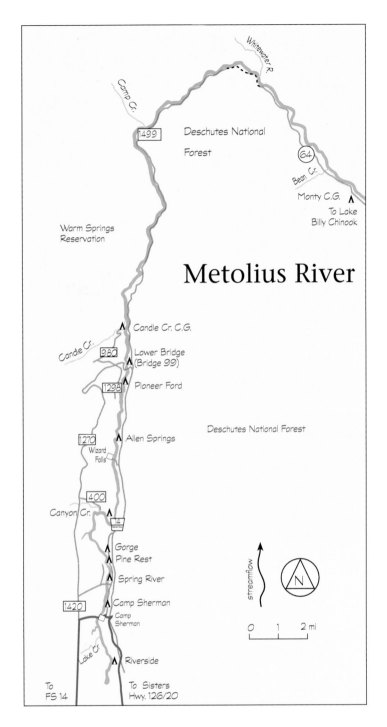

Metolius River

Services

Visitor facilities can be found in Camp Sherman, Black Butte, and Sisters. The Fly Fishers Place in Sisters is a good source for advice, flies, and tackle. The shops in Bend are also good sources, and some flies and tackle can be found at the Camp Sherman store. Forest Service regulations do not allow fishing guides on the Metolius.

Hatches and Other Food

The cold, constant river temperature, the even flow of water, and the micro-climates of different parts of the Metolius combine to give it the most varied and complex hatches in Oregon. Several anglers have attempted to catalog them by river section, but soon recognized the monumental nature of the task. The best advice is: "Be prepared for anything." Here are some of the main events.

Golden Stoneflies. The upper river is especially rich in these large stoneflies. They can hatch anytime between April and October, but June is the heaviest month.

Blue-Winged Olives. November through April these mayflies hatch around 1:00 p.m. When they aren't hatching and it's winter, present a small Gold Ribbed Hares Ear near the bottom.

Green Drakes. This big mayfly hatches early May through early June around 2:00-4:00 p.m. Nymphs can be productive a few hours before the hatch, but it's more fun to watch trout sip a big dry fly. A hatch of smaller green drakes happens in fall.

Caddis. Green rock worms, spotted caddis, and October caddis are common. The October caddis often shows up in late spring as well as fall.

Other Hatches. Salmonflies are a late May, early June event. The usual caddis hatches occur, as well as pale morning duns. Little yellow stoneflies are often seen in July, and olive stones can make a September appearance. The tiny black stonefly can be on the water in winter; a size 16-20 Elk Hair Caddis with a black body and black wing makes a good imitation.

aren't a lot of places for trout to rest. However, it is a rich river, so when you find fish they will be large and in good condition.

Whitefish are also common, and both kokanee and bull trout come up from Lake Billy Chinook to spawn in the fall. The kokanee die after spawning, but the bull trout do not. They linger in the river through winter and provide a fly fishing opportunity.

Fishing Tips

Long, thin leaders. A 12- to 15-foot leader tapered to 6X or 7X, even for big flies.

Sleep in. Metolius trout are seldom active before 10:00 a.m. Sometimes evening hatches are great, but most anglers give up before that. In winter, the best fishing is noon to 3:30.

Set your expectations. This is a tough river to pull many fish out of. If you get more than four in a day, you're doing well.

Pick your spots. The Metolius flows quickly, and fish need a reason to be in a certain place. Look carefully for ledges, backeddies, seams between fast and slow water, and places where the river slows and drops. As Jeff Perin at The Fly Fisher's Place says, "Some places consistently do *not* hold fish."

Avoid wading. Trout are often along the edges of the river. Don't wade until you've thoroughly explored the good water close to the bank.

Skip the shallow places. The campground area along the upper river near Camp Sherman is pretty, but it's shallow. The better fishing is below Pine Rest Campground as the river begins to deepen.

Go for the cripples. Patterns imitating cripples

Green drake season: a wild iris blooms beside a Metolius trail

and hatching duns are good anywhere, but especially on the Metolius due to the clarity of the water and the fishing pressure. X-Caddis, Floating Nymphs, Knocked Down Duns, etc. are good choices.

Special Regulations

Fly-fishing-only above Bridge 99. Artificial flies and lures only below Bridge 99. Catch-and-release only for all fish. All tributaries closed except Lake Creek.

Crooked River

This is one of the most productive trout streams in Oregon. Each river mile below Bowman Dam holds over 6,000 wild native rainbow trout that exceed eight inches. If you like the prospect of catching dozens of trout in a day, this is the place to come. While the typical trout is not large (10-12 inches), there are fish over 20 inches. The river is moderately alkaline, which is why it is rich and supports so many trout.

The Crooked River drains a wide area, but most of the fishing is focused on the seven miles below Bowman Dam. The dam keeps the water cool, but it also keeps it muddy. Upstream habitat degradation results in large amounts of clay being washed into Prineville Reservoir. The clay dissolves in water and stays in suspension, so the Crooked runs turbid most of the time. The trout are used to it, however, and anglers should not be turned off if the river has a brown tinge.

The Crooked, Metolius, and Deschutes rivers join forces to make the lower Deschutes. Like the Deschutes, the Crooked is a desert river, and the stretch below Bowman Dam flows through a deep lava canyon. Unlike many rivers, the Crooked fishes best fall through spring. Go somewhere else for your summer fishing, but consider the Crooked River the rest of the year.

Access and Facilities

From Hwy. 26 in Prineville, follow the signs to Bowman Dam. The turn-off is in the middle of Prineville. You should be on Hwy. 27 (do *not* take the road to Prineville Reservoir). The dam is about 20 miles from town. Fishing is concentrated on seven miles of public land between Bowman Dam and Hoffman Dam (just upstream from Castle Rock Campground).

Hwy. 27 hugs the east bank, and trails give access everywhere terrain permits. The banks are open and grassy, so casting is easy. There are many places a careful wader can cross the river, flows permitting, and fish the west bank.

Within this stretch there are nine BLM campgrounds and three picnic areas.

Species

Rainbow trout are the only gamefish. This is a self-sustaining population of native redband trout, a sub-species adapted to water temperatures and alkalinity that would kill most other trout. Whitefish (some quite large) are also present.

When to Fish

The river is open all year, but the best fishing is September to mid-May. June through mid-August, find another river. Winter fishing is excellent.

Services

Prineville is a big town, at least for this part of Oregon, with motels, restaurants, and other services for travelers. There is a small

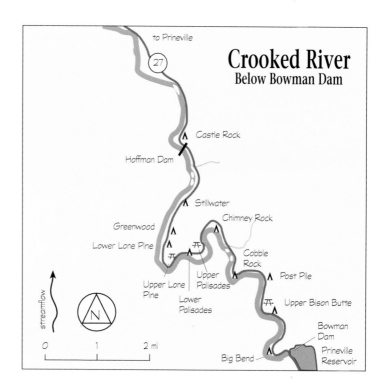

fly shop in Prineville; otherwise, the closest shops are in Bend and Sisters.

Hatches and Other Food

The primary winter trout food is blue-winged olive mayflies (*Baetis*), scuds, and midges. When fishing scuds, a fly with an orange tint works best in winter. When fishing *Baetis* patterns, don't just fish a dry fly. Often the larger fish are feeding on nymphs (see below).

Other hatches include mahogany duns (late summer), and caddis (late summer).

Fishing Tips

Winter turbidity. The river tends to be murky, even opaque, in winter. Don't be afraid of a sunken fly, however. I've had trout consistently hit a size 18 Pheasant Tail Nymph fished right on the bottom in three feet of water—and visibility (to me) was less than two inches at the surface.

Use light gear. This is a good river for light tackle rigs, such as three-weight rods.

Bankers' hours in winter. Like most good winter fly fishing rivers, the Crooked is best from late morning to mid-afternoon. The edges of the day are rarely productive.

Beadhead *Grammarus-Hyalella* Scud
(Randall Kaufmann)

Hook:	2457 or 200R, sizes 10-18
Thread:	To match body
Tail:	Marabou, hen hackle fibers, or antron; color to match body
Antennae:	Same as tail
Back:	Heavy plastic with pearl Flashabou underneath
Rib:	Clear monofilament, about .006 inch diameter
Body:	Blended angora goat and Haretron. When done tying, pick out body fibers to look like legs, then trim to correct length. Color choices: olive-gray, tan, orange.

Scuds should be slightly weighted either with lead under the body or a beadhead. The 2457 is a curved hook and represents a resting or drifting scud. The 200R hook is straighter and is used for a swimming scud. Match your presentation to the hook style.

Slow down and look. Rising trout can be tough to spot in winter. The small size of the insects (blue-winged olives and midges) means trout often make slow, sipping rises, especially in the slower water near shore. Murky brown water compounds the situation. So don't just slow down; come to a complete halt, then spend some time carefully examining the water. You might be surprised at how much is happening only 15 feet from the bank.

Special Regulations

Catch-and-release only for trout, and artificial flies and lures only, *except* from fourth Saturday in April through October 31.

Williamson River

There are very few rivers in North America where you can cast your fly and have a reasonable prospect of it being inhaled by a ten-pound wild trout. This is one of them.

While the river offers the opportunity for big trout, it does not yield its bounty easily. I consider it the most difficult trout river in Oregon. And when you do hook a big fish, there's no guarantee of landing it. That's why the most common fishing report is, "Hooked a big one, but he broke off."

Upper Klamath Lake is the engine that drives the Williamson River's fishing. Huge fish come up from the lake in search of better water conditions. The lake is rich, and the trout are naturally long-lived, so they spend a lot of time eating and growing enormous.

Access and Facilities

For most of the season, the best fly fishing is between the Chiloquin put-in and the Hwy.

97 bridge, about five miles. The put-in is off the south Chiloquin exit from Hwy. 97 (near milepost 249); look for a blue Klamath County Park sign, and don't expect too much. The boat slide is short but steep, and without four-wheel-drive you could get stuck. Contact Williamson River Anglers for a shuttle.

Except for the put-in, the riverbank is all private property, so you must have a white-water boat. The upper section has some very shallow, ledgey riffles that require good maneuvering and river-reading skills. The lower part is slow-moving "frog water," but it can have excellent fishing. The take-out is on private land across from the fly shop or at the Waterwheel RV park just downstream from the Hwy. 97 bridge (both charge a fee).

Motor boats can ply the river between the Hwy. 97 bridge and the lake. Between Modoc Rd. bridge and Waterwheel RV Park

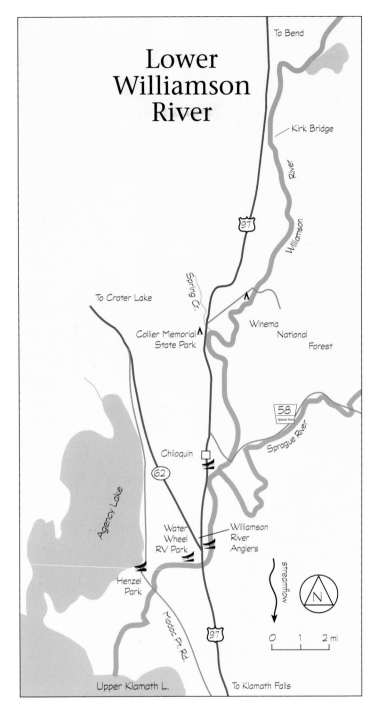

Lower Williamson River

To Bend

Kirk Bridge

River

US 97

Williamson

To Crater Lake

Spring Cr.

Collier Memorial
State Park

Winema   National
Forest

58

Sprague River

Chiloquin

62

Agency Lake

Water
Wheel
RV Park

Williamson
River
Anglers

streamflow

N

0   1   2 mi

Henzel
Park

Modoc Pt. Rd.

97

Upper Klamath L.

To Klamath Falls

---

there is a riffle that is impassable to up-stream-bound boats. Put-ins are at the Waterwheel and at Sportsman's RV park; there is a fee for each. Except during the *Hexagenia* hatch, most of this stretch is not good fly water, being mostly ill-defined and deep.

September to mid-October, you can sometimes find good fishing above Chil-oquin, but you can't fish from a boat above Chiloquin Bridge, and most of the riverbank is private property. Above Collier State Park, the river is quite small.

Bank anglers will have a tough time on the Williamson, but here are a few places that have access to the river: Waterwheel RV Park, Chiloquin put-in, under Hwy. 97 bridge, Collier State Park. All of these are very limited in scope.

Some maps show a road along the lower river's west bank. This is private property, and the landowners vigorously defend their rights.

Collier State Park has showers, RV hook-ups, and camping spaces not very many feet apart. Williamson River Campground, a Forest Service facility, is more spacious and pleasant for tent campers. It lacks plumbing, but it's less than half the cost of Collier, and anyone can shower at Collier for a couple of bucks. The river borders the Forest Service campground, but it's quite small, and the big fish (the reason people come to the Williamson) are farther downstream.

Species

The river supports big trout, most of them wild native rainbows with a few wild (but not native) brown trout. The biggest trout are those that spend most of their time in Upper Klamath Lake, where they can grow to 20 inches in three years and often reach ten pounds in a couple more years. The Klamath strain of rainbows are naturally long-lived. This, combined with the rich feed in the lake, makes for unusually large fish.

As the lake warms, its oxygen content plummets and its alkalinity soars. Beginning in mid-June, trout move into the rivers in search of better conditions. Or maybe not. If the lake is high and the summer is cool, the fish may stay in the lake.

When the trout first move into the river, they have an anchor worm on their skin. These parasites (called "cocopods" by local anglers) fall off after a couple of weeks in the river. To dislodge the parasites, trout will often jump and splash around.

When to Fish

Fishing is best mid-June through mid-October.

Services

There are visitor facilities along Hwy. 97, with everything you might need a bit farther south in Klamath Falls. Chiloquin has groceries and gas.

Williamson River Anglers on Hwy. 97 is a good source of flies, tackle, and information.

Hatches and Other Food

Hex (Hexagenia limbata). This giant yellow mayfly hatches in early July. While nymphs can be productive, most anglers can't resist using a dry fly. The hatch is in the slow-water area below the Chiloquin put-in; this is also a good time to fish the river below the Hwy. 97 bridge. *Hexagenias* need bankside vegetation, so you usually find concentrations of them where the riverbank is lined with willows.

Midges. This is a common hatch most days. You must get a sample of the natural insect and match it in size and color; otherwise you will have a frustrating and fishless day. The trout feed on blood midges in the lake and remain receptive to the pattern in the river. A red Serendipity can be effective, even when retrieved subsurface and in an unnatural manner.

Pale Morning Duns. PMDs are common in June, July, and even into August.

Tricos. The "tiny white-winged curse," Tricos are the source of many August and September hatches, and the source of much angling frustration. Long leaders, 6X or 7X tippets, and a high-riding dry fly are needed. And patience.

Caddis. Small flies usually work best for most hatches. The big October caddis makes an appearance, but not always in October.

Blue-winged olives. These are common near the end of the season.

Other food. The migratory trout are used to feeding on leeches, dragonfly nymphs, and

An angler plays a Williamson River trout on a cold fall morning.

baitfish in the lake. They continue to take imitations in the river.

Fishing Tips

Not a dry fly river. Except during the *Hexagenia* season, leech patterns, Woolly Buggers, and streamer flies such as Zonkers catch more big fish than anything else. Olive, brown, and black can be productive colors. The flies are usually fished down-and-across on a sinking line. The standard retrieve is a two-inch pull followed by a two-second pause; hits usually come during the pause.

Read the water carefully. The river is ledgey, with sudden drops and breaks. Bigger fish often lie in these spots, but if you aren't familiar with the river you may stumble onto the best places after you've already spooked the fish out of them. This is especially true for those fishing from boats below Chiloquin.

Favored lies. Trout are often found near the bank in 3-4 feet of water if there is deep water nearby. Other favored lies are near willow tangles, alongside ledges, and in troughs.

Clear water, tough choices. The water is clear, the fish are wary and big. Use too light a tippet, and you risk losing the fish. Too heavy, and you won't hook them. Most anglers use a long (at least 14 feet) leader tapered to 6X for dry flies, and 5X for wets; 4X can work for a wet fly if the light is low.

Hexagenia Paradrake
(Carl Richards and Doug Swisher)

Hook: 900BL, sizes 6-10
Thread: Yellow
Wing: Deer or elk hair, dyed gray. Wing should appear wide from side, narrow from front.
Tail: Moose
Rib: Yellow thread
Body: Deer or elk dyed yellow. Tie in front of wing, with hairs facing forward, and wrap up to hook eye. Then pull hair back along hook shank to make an extended body. Wrap with thread from head to tail.
Hackle: Grizzly dyed gold-tan and tied parachute style

Guides are good. This is a tough river for first timers, even if they are expert fly anglers. There are several excellent guides who can save you a lot of frustration. Use one your first day or two on the river so you get an idea of where the good spots are and how to approach the fish.

Conditions vary. There are many variables that affect the fishing here. Check with Williamson River Anglers for the current conditions before you come down.

Two anchors. Slow current means you need both stern and bow anchors to hold a boat in place.

Fish it for all it's worth. There is so much good water, and it needs to be fished so carefully, that you can easily spend 10-12 hours fishing the five-mile drift below Chiloquin.

Set your expectations. The potential rewards are great, but make no mistake: this is a tough river to fish well, perhaps the toughest in the state. A good day is half a dozen 14-17 inchers, and maybe two grabs from a big fish, one of which will break you off.

Special Regulations

Artificial flies and lures only.

Between Modoc Point Rd. Bridge and Chiloquin Bridge. No angling from a boat while the motor is running. One trout per day bag limit from fourth Saturday in May through July 31. From August 1 to October 31, catch-and-release only.

Between Chiloquin Bridge and Kirk Bridge. Same as above, except no fishing from a floating device, and no limit on brook trout.

Spooky fish. The big guys are easily put down. You need to stay 60-70 feet away and cast to a place you strongly suspect holds fish. Two or three casts is usually all you'll get before the fish are spooked off. Practice casting at home, not on the river.

McKenzie River

While not a "big fish" river, the McKenzie has many charms: beauty, wild fish, and proximity. It is more productive than most west-side trout streams, and native fish of 15 inches or more are common.

The McKenzie is a major tributary of the Willamette River, which it joins just north of Eugene. Private property makes this a boater's river, and the McKenzie-style drift boats you often see floating the river took their name from this stream. Most of the rapids are class II or lower, so only intermediate boating skills are needed. There is only one class IV, and it can be avoided if you pick your put-in and take-out spots.

Most of the trout fishing takes place below Blue River. Fishing can be good much of the year, and the spring March brown

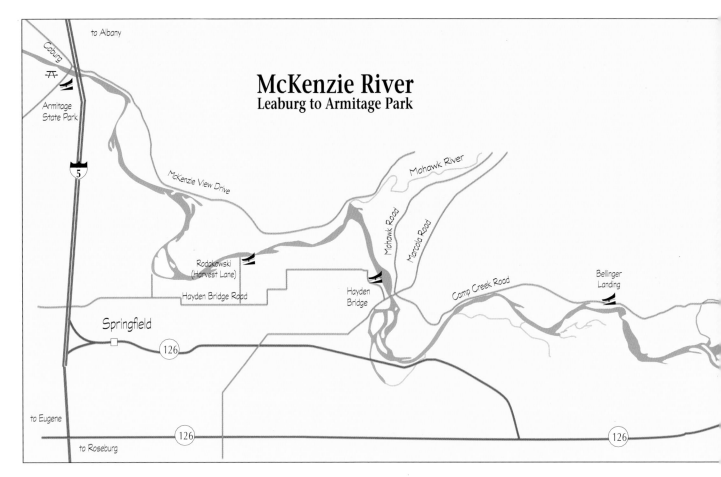

McKenzie River
Leaburg to Armitage Park

hatch is eagerly anticipated by fly anglers suffering from cabin fever and winter blahs.

Access and Facilities

Bank access to the McKenzie is extremely limited due to private property on both sides of the river. If you don't have a whitewater boat (or know someone with a riverside home), you'll have a tough time fishing this part of the McKenzie. Hwy. 126 parallels much of the river, and there are a few turnouts and parks where you could stop and cast a fly. Try also the 200 yards just east of I-5 on the north bank, and just below Leaburg Dam on the south bank.

For boaters, however, access is simple, and there are frequent boat ramps. Most of the McKenzie can be drifted by someone with intermediate whitewater talents, however Martin Rapids is class IV and requires more advanced skills. Most boat ramps have signs on Hwy. 126. The map shows their locations. Here are notes on a few of them.

Finn Rock. A popular put-in for rafters.

Rosborough. Above Nimrod. Cross an old wooden bridge to find a gravel ramp courtesy of Rosborough Lumber. No sign on Hwy. 126.

Silver Creek. Has a handicap platform.

Ben and Kay Dorris State Park. This is a good spot to take out and avoid Martin Rapids (class IV).

Helfrich. Down a paved road through an orchard. This is the first put-in after Martin Rapids.

Below Goodpasture covered bridge, you are on the lake behind Leaburg dam. There are two take-outs on the lake. Use Waterford Park on the south (left) bank; the other take-out is too close to the highway to be safe.

Deerhorn County Park. Turn down Holden Creek Lane, and cross the bridge. Turn into the wide parking area for the park, then drive under the bridge. The paved ramp is

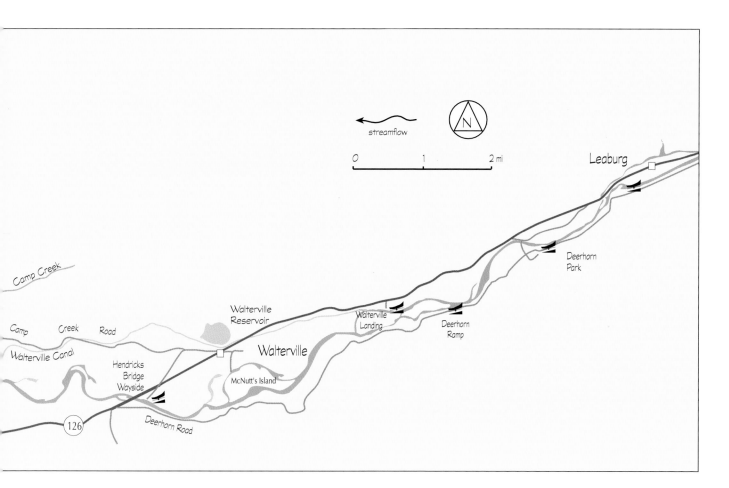

just downstream from the bridge.

Walterville. Look for a gravel drive off Hwy. 126 near the school. The paved ramp is on the EWEB canal, so this is a take-out only, not a launching point.

Hayden Bridge. A paved ramp with loads of parking on the south side of the river.

Rodakowski (Harvest Ln). Between here and the mouth it's all frog water. Most fly fishers pull out here rather than at Armitage.

Armitage. I-5 doesn't have a southbound off-ramp at Armitage, so if you're coming from the north take the Coburg exit.

When to Fish

Below Leaburg Dam, the McKenzie is open all year. Fishing can be particularly good in spring. The March brown hatch is eagerly anticipated by many anglers, and the May caddis hatches can be outstanding. Summer evenings are often good.

Species

Some rainbow trout are stocked, but there are many wild native rainbows. They closely resemble the Deschutes redsides, although biologists don't think they are the same strain of fish. Rainbows average 12 inches, but there are many that are 15 inches or more. Native cutthroat are also present and are especially thick below Hayden Bridge.

Services

The Eugene/Springfield metro area is nearby and has everything you could possible want, and a great deal you probably don't. There are fly shops in Eugene and Salem.

Hatches and Other Food

March Browns. This early spring event is one of the most anticipated hatches on the river. The best hatches occur on drippy days. They begin around 1:00 and last about an hour, if you're lucky and have crummy weather.

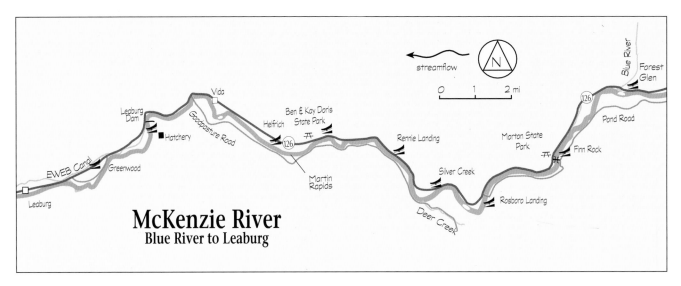

McKenzie River
Blue River to Leaburg

Elk Hair Caddis
(Al Troth)

Hook:	900BL, sizes 10-20
Thread:	To match body
Rib:	Fine copper wire
Body:	Antron or Haretron
Hackle:	Natural or dyed grizzly, palmered
Wing:	Natural elk

Tie this fly in these combinations: tan body with natural grizzly hackle and tan elk hair wing; olive body with olive dyed grizzly hackle and tan elk hair wing; black body with black hackle and dark elk hair wing. Most caddis are matched with size 14-18 hooks.

When casting to rough, water you need the hackle. The rest of the time, I clip the underside hackle very short so the fly will ride lower in the water.

McKenzie Caddis. This big caddis hatches in spring. The body is bright green. The females dive below the surface to lay their eggs. When you see this happening, tie on a Soft Hackle or a Diving Caddis and present it on a wet-fly swing.

Little Yellow Stonefly. This July hatch runs contrary to the usual stonefly habits: the adults emerge in the water, like mayflies, and not on land like other self-respecting stoneflies. A yellow-bodied size 12 Soft Hackle works well when presented down-and-across on a wet-fly swing.

Other hatches. November through February, blue-winged olives dominate the water. Midges are also common, and pale morning duns make a June appearance. Green drakes may appear in June, and a smattering of yellow quills in late June. It is a caddis-rich river, however, and some species or other of caddis will be hatching just about any day of the year.

Fishing tips

Soft Hackles work well. As in most caddis-rich rivers, Soft Hackle patterns are very effective and easy to fish. Choose a size and color appropriate to the season's hatches (see the chart in the back of this book). Cast at a 45-60 degree angle downstream, mend line upstream to slow the drift, and let the fly swing across in the current. It's a simplistic way to fish, but it catches a lot of trout.

Egg patterns in December. The last month of the year is when whitefish spawn. Trout are eager for the roe, and a small, pink egg fly tossed in behind spawning whitefish will often pick up a trout.

Cutthroats like slow water. Languid, almost stagnant water—especially when overhung with alder branches— is a favorite spot for the river's native cutthroat.

There's more to the McKenzie than the McKenzie. Good fishing doesn't end at the river's confluence with the Willamette. A few anglers start their trip on the McKenzie at Armitage Park, but keep right on drifting into the Willamette and take out at Hays Rd. (a distance of about 11 miles). This part of the Willamette has excellent fly fishing for wild trout. And no competition.

Special Regulations

Only fin-clipped trout may be kept.

Below Hayden Bridge. Artificial flies and lures only.

Between Leaburg Dam and Hayden Bridge. Artificial flies and lures only, *except* from fourth Saturday in April through October 31.

Owyhee River

If you check out the license plates of anglers who park their cars along the Owyhee River, you'll notice that most of them came from Idaho. Hardly anyone from Oregon fishes here, which is a pity. Of course, for most of us it's a long, long drive, whereas Boise anglers can leave after work and still fish the evening rise.

There are really two Owyhee Rivers. The upper river flows through spectacular desert rock formations. It is remote and rugged, and is an excellent smallmouth bass fishery. Below Lake Owyhee, however, the river is completely different. While you are still in a canyon, the river is cooler and supports rainbow and brown trout. Some of those browns are very big indeed, and I've seen them take everything from a size 20 *Baetis* Paradun to a size 2 Woolly Bugger.

In summer, the river flows cold and high as water is released from the dam for irrigators. And in winter, the Owyhee is often frozen over. But in spring and fall, fishing can be excellent.

If you've got the time and the wanderlust, this is a worthy journey. If it's a long drive for you, think about the salmon. Until habitat degradation and overfishing made the runs a memory, salmon swam up the Columbia and Snake rivers, then used the Owhyee as a highway into Nevada.

Access and Facilities

From Ontario, follow the signs first for Nyssa, then for Lake Owyhee. This puts you on Hwy. 201. Take Hwy. 201 south from Nyssa, and follow signs for Lake Owyhee. Before

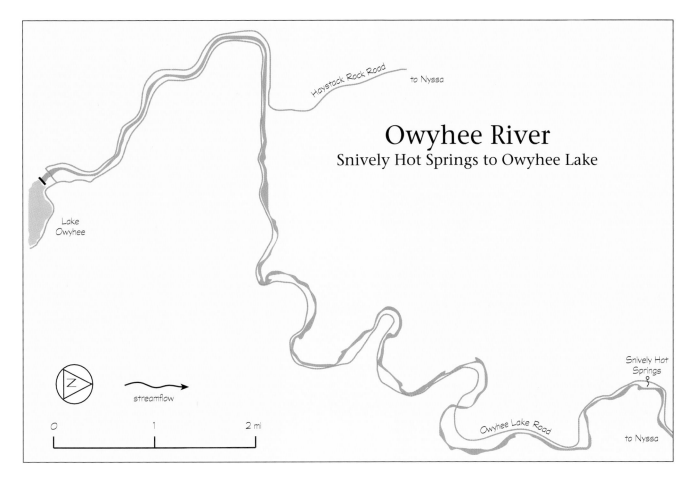

Owyhee River
Snively Hot Springs to Owyhee Lake

you reach the lake you will come to Snively Hot Springs (you gotta love these names). Upstream from Snively, the road parallels the river. Between Snively and the dam, there are 13 miles of river bank, most of which is public land.

There is excellent bank access, and you can wade across the river in many places. Boats are not appropriate on this river.

Lake Owyhee State Park is a few miles above the dam. It has camping and picnicking facilities. You can also camp near the river at just about any point, but there are no facilities.

Species

The lower Owyhee holds rainbow and brown trout. The typical rainbow is 12 inches. The average brown goes 16-18 inches, but there are fish over five pounds. Rainbows are stocked annually, browns every other year.

When to Fish

Summer flows are high and cold, and in winter the river is often iced over. Early spring can be excellent if you get here between ice-out and April 15 (when irrigation starts). July through October can be quite good, es-

The lower Owyhee is a series of quiet pools with occasional riffles.

Parachute Baetis
(Pret Frazier)

Hook: 900BL, sizes 16-22
Thread: Olive
Wing: Mallard flank, tied parachute style
Tail: Two blue dun Micro Fibbets, split
Body: Olive Haretron or Superfine
Hackle: Natural or olive-dyed grizzly

pecially after the end of irrigation in mid-October.

Services

Vale and Nyssa have some services, but Ontario is the best bet for decent motels, restaurants, and other visitor services.

Hatches and other food

The standard northwest hatches happen here. Midges can come off at any time. Blue-winged olives are common fall through spring. Mahogany duns are abundant in fall. Leeches, crayfish, snails (I never met anyone who could honestly claim to catch a lot of fish on a snail pattern), and small fish are also common forage.

Fishing Tips

Conditions vary. River flow is managed for irrigation, not fishing. It will vary depending on the season. Some of the highest, coldest flows are in summer.

Fish lies will change. Fish will be in different places depending on river level. This is especially true of browns. They will be in slack water, but you will find slack water in different places depending on river flow.

Slow stretches for browns. Most people's first reaction to the lower Owyhee is, "Huh?" The river is a series of slow or stagnant pools with occasional riffles. Don't worry about it. I think nearly every one of these slow pools holds at least one brown trout over four pounds. Find slackwater areas that are two feet deep or more. If there are no rises, fish the pools with streamers such as Matukas, leech patterns, Woolly Buggers, or Zonkers. Fish your fly near the bottom on a sinking line.

Brown trout are not nice people. Brown trout are lazy, greedy cannibals. If they were people, you wouldn't want to know one. I met an angler who landed a 23-inch brown on this river; it had an 11-inch rainbow in its mouth. That tells you what big browns are looking for when the hatch isn't on.

Turbidity will hide your leader. The Owyhee often runs brown and murky, which helps hide your leader. For subsurface fishing, you can get away with a 3X tippet. When the river drops and clears at the end of the irrigation season, go to a thinner tippet.

Heads of pools. At the head (upstream end) of most pools, you will find trout slurping food that drifts down to them. They will usually be some of the biggest trout in the pool.

Riffles for more rainbows. While some of the slow water holds large rainbows, you should find plenty of 10-14 inch fish in the riffly areas.

Special Regulations

Brown trout must be released unharmed.

Wood River

The Wood is a meandering, spring-fed river running down the west side of the Klamath Valley and emptying into Agency Lake. The river is seldom more than 30-feet wide, and is often shallow. Yet big wild browns and rainbows are caught here, most of them well over six pounds.

Like it's near neighbor, the Williamson River, the Wood's fishing is fueled by Upper Klamath Lake. Shallow and rich, the lake nourishes big trout, then becomes too warm and alkaline for them. Fish migrate to the rivers in search of better water conditions.

Much of the Wood River is surrounded by private land, so it's difficult to fish it without a boat. The most common float is the 12-mile drift from Weed Rd. Bridge to the mouth. Fishing is strictly catch-and-release, artificial flies and lures only.

Access and Facilities

There is over a quarter-mile of public bank access at the Wood River Day Use Area off Sun Mountain Rd. This national forest site has two handicapped platforms, toilets, and tables. It's possible to launch a small, untrailered boat here. There is a small amount of bank access at the Weed Rd. bridge. The lower 1.5 miles of the Wood now flows through public land; motor vehicles are not permitted, but walkers (some carrying float tubes) and mountain bikers are welcome.

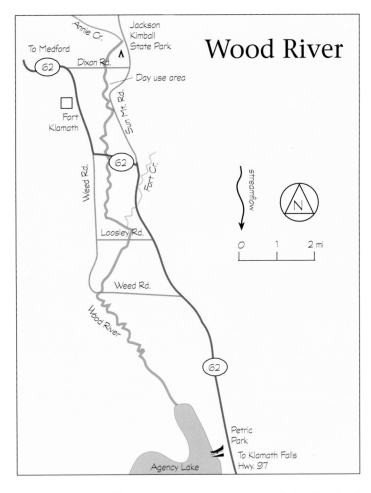

Species

Both rainbow and brown trout are present. Some are resident fish, but the biggest trout are migrants who move up from the lake in the fall in search of cool water or spawning gravel. Migratory fish begin entering the Wood in June, and fresh fish will nose in as late as February.

When to Fish

Fishing begins as early as June, but it's a bit slow until the hopper season in August. By September, migratory fish enter the river in earnest and work their way upstream. The river is closed after October 31.

Services

Motels and restaurants are on US 97, and there are some facilities in Fort Klamath, Chiloquin, and at Rocky Point (see the chapter on Upper Klamath Lake). Klamath Falls has more extensive visitor services, but it is almost an hour's drive from the Wood.

Two excellent fishing lodges in the area are CrystalWood Lodge (541/381-2322) and Horseshoe Ranch (541/381-2297). Both have access to private water.

Williamson River Anglers on US 97 near Chiloquin is a good fly shop.

Hatches and Other Food

There are hatches of midges, blue-winged olives, and caddis in the fall, but unless there is a hatch that generates rising fish, most anglers either fish a grasshopper pattern (in August) or a large streamer. Most of the river's fish are predatory monsters that have moved up from the lake. They like a big meal, so Bunny Leeches and big weighted Matukas or Woolly Buggers are what usually get tied on.

Fishing Tips

You need a boat. Unless you have access to private water, most of the Wood requires a boat of some kind. Anglers drift from bridge to bridge, or from Weed Rd. to the mouth (take out at Petric Park). The bridges aren't high enough to get a boat under, so you need

There are two ways around the limited access problem: stay at a lodge that has private access, such as Horseshoe Ranch, or float the river. Small boats such as pontoon craft can be launched at the bridges (except Dixon). Trailered craft such as drift boats can be launched at a rough slide at the Weed Rd. bridge. Although the Wood is not a whitewater river, it can be deceptively fast and has occasional snags. River drifters need to be good at reading the current and at anticipating problem areas. Because the riverbank is almost all private, you must stay in your boat. Drifting the river works best with two or more people so one can row while the others fish. Arrange shuttles through Williamson River Anglers.

Campers can stay at Kimball State Park on Sun Mountain Rd. It's small and has limited facilities (no plumbing, for example), but it's cheap for a state park and is near the headwaters of the Wood.

a pontoon boat you can pick up and carry if you are above the Weed Rd. bridge. At Weed, there is a rough dirt slide from which a drift boat can be launched and floated to the mouth of the river, a distance of about 12 miles. It takes all day; many boaters carry a small electric motor for the final miles.

August is hopper season. In August, use a floating line with a nine-foot leader tapered to 2X. Cast a hopper pattern along the margins near grassy areas.

Twisty river makes for undercuts and holes. The Wood is a low-gradient river that meanders sinuously through flat pasture land. There is deep water on the outside of most turns, and in many cases there is an undercut bank. This is where most fish will be lying.

Sink-tip line. Other than the hopper season, you need a fly line with a 20-foot or so sink tip. Not a floater with lead on the leader, and not a full-sinker. A sink-tip. Tie on about 4 feet of eight-pound leader, then a weighted fly. You need to be down deep in the holes.

Presentation. Cast your streamer near the bank at the upstream end of each turn and dead drift it or slowly retrieve it through the deeper water. And hang on.

It's not the Williamson. People who haven't been here often lump the Wood and the Williamson together. They are completely different rivers, even though they are near each other. The Wood is narrower, has a different bottom, twists more, has a hopper season, is a much longer boat trip, is fished differently, and its trout are not as spooky. They're both great rivers with monstrous wild trout, but they are not fished in the same way at all.

Set your expectations. You are unlikely to hook many fish on the Wood. Two a day is doing well. You might not hook any. And if you do hook a fish, it is more likely to break off than to be landed. But when you hook

Henry's Fork Hopper
(Mike Lawson)

Hook:	5212, size 6-14
Thread:	Yellow
Body:	Light elk hair. Use hair about three times the length of the hook shank. Wrap with thread from where the wing ties in to past hook bend, then pull forward and wrap back to the beginning point.
Underwing:	Yellow elk
Overwing:	Mottled brown hen saddle, wide and round. Treat with Flexament and shape with your fingers.
Head:	Light elk, same length as hook shank. Tied bullet style with ends facing back, over wings, to make a collar. Trim the underside close to the body.
Legs:	Round yellow rubber. Tie knots in the middle.

one of the Wood's big trout, you have the pleasure of knowing you connected to one of the largest wild trout in North America.

Special Regulations

Artificial flies and lures only. All trout must be released unharmed.

Fall River

An angler I know rented a cabin on Fall River for a September weekend with his wife. Saturday afternoon he caught a 23-inch rainbow trout and a 25-inch brown—both wild fish and both hooked on dry flies. He came back to the cabin on an emotional high, and a couple of hours later his first son was conceived.

Not every day on Fall River is like that, however. For one thing, the fish are rarely that large. It's not a "big fish" river, but it is spring-fed and flows through a pretty setting of large pines. The water is cold and clear, trout can be plentiful, and many Oregon fly anglers got their start here. Fall River has definite charms.

The river is about seven miles long. Four miles downstream from the springs that feed it, there is a large falls. The falls blocks migra-

tion of brown and rainbow trout from the upper Deschutes, who come into the Fall River searching for cool flows and spawning habitat. The river closes early below the falls to protect these fish.

Above the falls, the river is now open year-round. Most fish in this stretch come from a hatchery that sits at the river's midpoint. Trout are stocked regularly, so fishing is often good near the hatchery grounds; it's a popular spot with anglers. Upstream from the hatchery, fish can still be found. They are less numerous, but are often larger and more wily than those near the hatchery.

Access and Facilities

FR 42 parallels the river from its source to the hatchery. There are several turn-outs with trails that lead to the river, and the entire stretch has a good trail along the north bank. There is a primitive campground (no drinking water) near the river's source. The hatchery itself is a popular starting place for anglers. You can fish on the hatchery grounds (in the river, not the broodstock tanks!), and from the trail that heads upstream.

Below the hatchery, FR 4360 crosses the river; you can park near the bridge and follow a trail down the north bank almost to the Deschutes. This section is part of the state La Pine Recreation Area, so it is public property. Other than the places mentioned above, most of Fall River's banks are private.

Species

Above the falls, catchable rainbow and brook trout (7-12 inches) are stocked almost weekly except in winter. Below the falls, large browns and rainbows sometimes come up from the Deschutes. Browns spawn in this stretch, so the river is closed below the falls after September 30.

When to Fish

Because it is spring-fed, Fall River changes little with the seasons. If you can get to it, you can fish it.

Services

Bend, La Pine, and Sunriver offer the nearest visitor facilities. There are fly shops in Bend and Sunriver.

Hatches and Other Food

Summer through fall, midges, caddis, pale morning duns, and pale evening duns are the primary hatches. October caddis are especially important in fall. There is a noted mid-summer hatch of mahogany duns. In winter, small midges (size 26 and 28) and blue-winged olives dominate. Stoneflies are rarely significant in this river.

Fishing Tips

Best times of day. As in most cold spring creeks, Fall River's trout need a few hours of daylight to stir them up. Fishing rarely begins before 10 a.m. Evening activity can be excellent, especially in summer.

Hatchery area popular. The hatchery grounds are quite popular, particularly with beginners and families. Frequent releases of catchable trout are part of the reason. If you are seeking a different kind of experience, head upstream or fish below the falls.

Fishing near the falls. The water just below the falls is productive. Cast a high-floating dry fly into the frothy water near the falls.

Adams
(Leonard Halladay)

Hook:	900BL, sizes 10-20
Thread:	Gray
Wing:	Grizzly hen hackle tips
Tail:	Grizzly, grizzly and brown hackle fibers, or moose hair (shown)
Body:	Gray Haretron or muskrat
Hackle:	Grizzly and brown hackle, wrapped together

A Female Adams is tied the same way, but with a small bit of yellow dubbing at the rear of the body to imitate a mayfly ready to lay eggs.

The Adams is the most generic dry fly; it resembles a lot of different kinds of trout food. While it is seldom the "right" fly (*Callibaetis* hatches are an exception), it is rarely the "wrong" fly. I usually tie on a fly that matches a specific hatch, but I always carry a bunch of Adams in sizes 12-20 (but mostly 14-18) for unknown or unusual hatches or as a dry fly to use when there is no hatch.

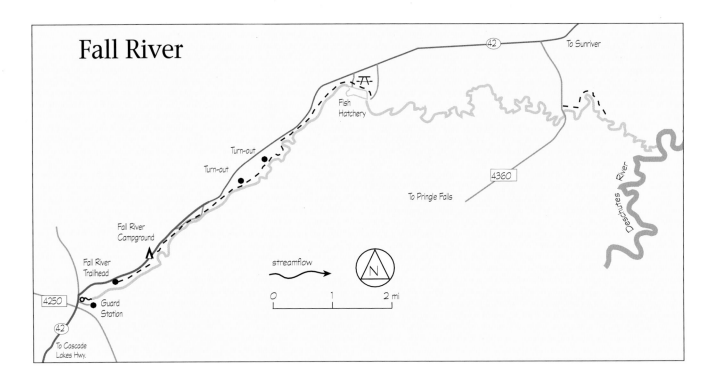

Fall River

Look for good holding water. Unless there's a hatch that draws fish onto the flats, concentrate your casts along grassy banks and logs, and near ledges, deep pools, and slots.

Don't take the fish for granted. It's amazing how a trout that's been raised on pellets in a concrete tank can become extremely selective about fly patterns after only a week in the river. Watch the insect activity carefully, and match what the fish are taking; size is most important, then color, then pattern.

Be stealthy. It's clear water, and the fish can spot you very easily. Crouch near the bank, avoid wading, be sneaky, and you will be rewarded with larger fish.

Special Regulations

Fly-fishing-only with barbless hooks.

Below the falls. Non-finclipped rainbow trout must be released unharmed. Open the fourth Saturday in April through September 30.

Above the falls. Open all year.

Rogue River "Holy Water"

It seems like every state has at least one tail-water trout fishery that locals call "The Holy Water." This is Oregon's. Admittedly, it has a few religious aspects: divine blessedness (in the size and number of trout); human reverence and adoration (of trout); annual pilgrimages (especially during salmonfly sea-son); and punishment (by the trout) for the deadly sins of impatience and bad casting.

The Rogue's "Holy Water" is a short fishery, barely half a mile long. It lies in a nice setting, if you ignore the concrete dam rising hundreds of feet at one end. Trout are numerous, and the typical fish is 16-17 inches

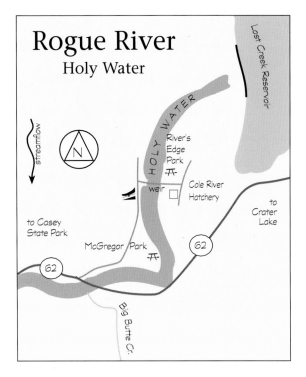

Rogue River

Holy Water

When to Fish

Fishing is good and accessible all year. The salmonfly hatch runs from late May through mid-June, and evening fishing can be superb but crowded.

Services

Shady Cove is a few miles west and has restaurants, motels, RV parks, and supplies. Medford, Ashland, and Grants Pass have extensive visitor facilities.

Some flies and tackle are at the Fishin' Hole in Shady Cove. There are full-service fly shops in Ashland and Medford.

Hatches and Other Food

Blue-Winged Olives. November through April; use size 18 and 20 dry flies.

Salmonflies. A major event from late May through mid-June; evening egg-laying swarms are awesome.

Caddis. May through July, and again in September and October; use size 16 and 18 Elk Hair Caddis in colors that match the prevailing insects.

Leeches. Leech patterns work well in July and August. Use a sinking line. Either quarter your cast downstream and let the fly swing across, or cast across stream and retrieve the fly in two-foot strips with a slight pause between each strip.

Other Hatches. A few March browns show up in March and early April, and green drakes can sometimes be found in late May.

Fishing tips

When it's crowded, give the water a rest. The busiest season here is the salmonfly hatch. Most evenings, anglers stack up near the dam and stand a cast apart; most never stop casting. Don't do it! Stake out your patch of water, then sit on a rock until you see fish rising near you. Then cast (downstream presentation) to a rising fish. After hooking and releasing your trout, go back to the rock until you see fish rising again. You'll fish less, but you'll catch more.

long, with fish over six pounds available (but hard to catch).

The May salmonfly hatch is a major event for local anglers, but the fishery is open all year for fly-fishing-only, catch-and-release angling.

Access and Facilities

Turn off Hwy. 62 at the sign for Cole M. Rivers Fish Hatchery. To reach the east bank, turn right at the weir and go to Rivers Edge Park; the river is a short stroll from the parking lot. To reach the west bank, bear left at the weir; park on the side of the road.

Rivers Edge Park is a pleasant, day-use-only facility with toilets and tables. The nearest camping is at Rogue Elk Park (on Hwy. 62 towards Shady Cove) and at Stewart State Park (off Hwy. 62 a few miles east of the Holy Water). Stewart is the quieter of the two.

Species

Rainbow trout are stocked as fingerlings. They are the only species here. Feed is ample, and with no competition from other species, they soon grow to good size. The average trout is about 16 inches, but I've seen anglers land fish that were over six pounds.

Downstream presentation. Most of the time, a downstream presentation works best because your fly reaches the trout before the leader and line.

Fish close to shore. It's a great temptation to cast to the middle of the river. It's rarely successful, though, and when you do it, your line passes over all the fish close to the bank—and puts them down. There are a lot of fish close to shore. Go for them.

Go light. Use a 12-foot leader tapered to 5X or even 6X.

Don't forget the lower end. Most anglers concentrate on the top third of the water, nearest the dam. However, there is good fishing throughout the Holy Water.

MacSalmon
(Al Troth)

Hook:	5263 or 200R, sizes 4-6
Thread:	Black to construct fly, but use fire orange floss to tie in legs at the end.
Abdomen:	Orange braided macrame cord. Thread onto hook, leaving some extending past the hook bend. Melt the end with a lighter.
Underwing:	A few strands of Krystal Flash (black and orange), then a No. 11 Shamazaki Fly Wing that extends beyond the abdomen.
Overwing:	Light elk hair and orange-dyed elk hair
Head:	Dark moose tied bullet style. Ends make a collar
Legs:	Black round rubber

Small Streams

From the Willamette Valley to the coast range to the desert, there are many small streams that offer a pleasant fishing experience. There are too many of them to mention by name, and I wouldn't tell you anyway (see the fishing tip, "Keep you mouth shut.)

You don't fish the creeks for trophies. While there are a few places you can pick up a 14-16 inch trout, in most of Oregon's small waters you should consider a ten-incher to be a trophy. The rewards are not big fish. They are scenery, quiet, solitude, and a host of other emotional and spiritual benefits.

In my experience, the people who most enjoy small stream fishing fall into two groups: beginners who want a "training water" on which to learn the basics of fly fishing, and experts who have caught enough big fish so they no longer feel a need to prove themselves and who are looking for a change of pace.

Here are some tips for finding and fishing Oregon's small streams.

Tackle and Flies

A light rod is best, such as a three- or four-weight. Since most casts are short, and backcast room is often limited, a short rod is a good choice. I use a seven-and-a-half foot four-weight. I prefer a fiberglass rod for small stream work because glass will load with less line than graphite, and most small stream casts are short.

Floating line is usually sufficient, and a 5X tippet will do for all but the clearest creeks. I usually use a seven-foot leader, again because most casts are short and backcast room is often limited; on an open creek in eastern Oregon, however, I'll switch to a longer leader.

The flies I carry are these: tan Elk Hair Caddis, Parachute Adams, and Pheasant Tail Nymph, all in sizes 14-18; Griffiths Gnat (size 20); olive Woolly Bugger (size 10); and a few Hares Ear Soft Hackles (brown bodies, sizes 14-18).

Finding Fish

In small streams, trout are found in predictable places: the heads of riffles (right in the white water), along ledges, in pools more than 18 inches deep with some current (not stagnant water); behind and alongside rocks; under fallen trees. In general, you'll find fish any place the water deepens and slows.

Some streams, however, have no fish. The water may be too shallow and fast, or too cold and sterile to support aquatic life. The best place to begin a search for good creek water is in *Fishing in Oregon*. Pick a few likely spots, and begin exploring. Exploration is half the fun of fishing creeks.

Fishing Tips

Forget the hippers. I either wear chest-high waders or, more often, Capilene long johns with a pair of nylon pants or shorts over them. The latter is good for "wet wading" in summer and early fall. I feel hip boots just tempt you into water that's too deep.

Access. Many small streams flow through private property, so finding public water will be a bigger challenge than finding trout. Many of the north coast creeks are on private timber land with gates across the road. However the gates are usually to keep cars and timber thieves out. Unless the land is clearly posted otherwise, it should be okay to walk down the road to a likely creek.

Wade upstream. Once I've put myself in the water, my usual approach is to wade up-

Hares Ear Nymph

Hook:	5262 or 3761, size 8-18
Thread:	Brown
Tail:	Hare's ear fur
Abdomen:	Blended hare's ear. Keep it thin.
Rib:	Gold mylar tinsel or copper wire
Wingcase:	Turkey tail coated with Flexament
Thorax:	Hares ear. After tying, pick out a few hairs so they look like legs.

This can be tied weighted or unweighted. A bead head works well, too. Dark brown is the most productive color; dark olive and tan can also work well. Some anglers use peacock herl for the thorax.

Winter anglers take note: when tied on a size 18 hook, a Hares Ear with dark brown dubbing and a gold mylar rib is an excellent imitation of a blue-winged olive nymph.

stream, casting to each pool and ledge as I come to it.

Keep it simple. Mobility is everything, so keep your gear to a minimum: a single box of flies, a spool of tippet material, floatant, nippers, forceps. If it won't fit into a shirt pocket or small shoulder bag, I don't take it.

Don't ignore wet flies. Many creek anglers think only in terms of dry flies, yet a well-fished wet can be very productive and will often yield bigger fish. A size 10 Woolly Bugger fished under a log or along a boulder can give surprising results.

Keep your mouth shut. Once you've found a good creek, don't tell the world. The way I look at it, the joy of small stream fishing is exploration and discovery. So you'd just be spoiling someone else's fun if you gave them precise directions to a good spot.

Other Rivers

Blitzen (Donner und Blitzen)

This desert river flows off Steens Mountain near Frenchglen and empties into Malheur Lake. Fishing can be good throughout, but the heaviest fish (and heaviest fishing pressure) are at the lower end near Page Springs Campground. While the fish decrease in size as you get farther from the river's mouth, the crowds also decrease. At the upper end of the river, you are into wild country with wild (but smallish) redband trout.

The lower part of the Blitzen can be reached from Page Springs Campground, which is near the town of Frenchglen on Hwy. 205. There is a trail that follows the river upstream. Watch for snakes.

The upper river is tough to get to. One way to reach it is from Steens Mountain Loop, which crosses the Blitzen 17 miles from Hwy. 205 (take Steens Mountain Loop 10 miles south of Frenchglen on Hwy. 205). At this crossing, the river is in a small canyon and is difficult to follow along its bank, although you can easily wade most of it. You can reach the Blitzen lower down by following spur roads off Steens Mountain Loop, however these roads are incredibly rough and rocky; I think you're better off walking up from Page Springs.

The Blitzen is best late in the year. Through July it can be too turbid for good fishing, and August is too darned hot out here. But fall fishing can be delightful. There are other creeks in the Steens area that are worth exploring, too.

Storms in this area can be sudden and violent. They are the source of the river's name, which is German for "thunder and lightning." (So how come we don't call the river "The Donner?") Another local hazard is rattlesnakes, which are quite common. And you are in remote country. For some anglers, the weather, snakes, and remoteness are all part of the Blitzen's appeal. For others, they are good reasons to go somewhere else.

Klamath River

Most of the Klamath flows through California, but it begins in Oregon, and some sections have excellent fishing. The river empties Upper Klamath Lake, but a series of dams leave only three short free-flowing sections in Oregon.

Link River. This vestigial part of the Klamath is between Upper Klamath Lake and Lake Ewauna, right in the town of Klamath Falls. Fishable water is limited, but it's not heavily used. Five-pound trout are available.

The upper end is reached from a parking area off Nevada Ave. Park, then walk through the turnstile. Follow a broad gravel path until you cross the canal on a bridge. Walk to the river through the trees. The other end is where Hwy. 97 crosses the river. Take the "City Center" exit off Hwy. 97. The parking area is off Main St. (look for signs for "Riverside School") on the west side.

Keno. Between Keno Dam and Boyle Reservoir there are six miles of good fishing for rainbow trout that often top five pounds. There is access to the upper end from the Keno Recreation Area off Hwy. 66. To reach the river farther down, take Hwy. 66 and park in a turn-out (there are several). It's a steep climb down the canyon to the river; it helps if some of your ancestors were mountain goats.

Another way in is to take Clover Creek Rd. off Hwy. 66 near Keno (where 66 makes a sharp turn). Turn right on Old Wagon Rd. (where Clover Creek Rd. starts up a hill); at the stop sign, turn right onto a two-lane gravel road. This is the Weyerhaeuser Rd.; if you see "PGT" signs, you're on the right road. Stop where the second set of power lines (the ones hung from steel, not wooden, towers) cross the road. Park off the road, and climb down the canyon. This is a slightly less athletic entry than off Hwy. 66.

Fish average 18-20 inches, with some over 30 inches. Throughout most of this

A Klamath River rainbow from the Keno stretch. They're not all this big.

which is known as the Frain Ranch. The rainbows are smaller than those in the Keno-Boyle stretch, but they are more numerous. To reach this water, turn off Hwy. 66 onto Klamath River Rd. where you see a sign for "John C. Boyle Powerhouse." You'll soon come to a fork in the road; take the upper fork, and keep on trucking until you're past the power house (a couple of miles). This is good road until you reach the put-in for the whitewater rafters. Then it turns very bumpy and slow. Drive as far as you can stand it, then park along the road and walk to the river.

There are lots of fat 10-14 inch fish in here. If the Williamson's big, spooky bruisers beat you up, come down here and salve your ego. Watch your step, though, because the rocks collect a lot of algae and make for tricky wading.

The dam governs the river here. River level varies throughout the day, with low flows in morning, then high flows during peak power generation times. Fishing is best during the low flows, but the fish are used to the fluctuating levels and are still catchable when the river is high.

Sprague River

The Sprague is a Williamson River tributary. The confluence is just above the boat launch at Chiloquin. The river is managed for wild trout, with rainbows, brooks, and browns available to anglers. The best action is in the lower Sprauge, where rainbows often reach three pounds or more.

From Hwy. 97, go into Chiloquin and take Hwy. 140 (Sprague River Rd.). There is access from this road near Chiloquin. At Chiloquin Ridge Rd., turn right (there's a power station there). A dirt road leads to the river just past the bridge. You can continue down Chiloquin Ridge Rd. to where you see a sign announcing "Pavement Ends." Before you reach the sign, turn right onto a single-lane gravel road. When it forks, go straight through the gate. This puts you on a rough road that gives access to the canyon section.

It is possible to drift this section in a small boat (canoe, pram, pontoon; anything

stretch, your best approach is to stand on a large rock (not wade), and tie on a large streamers, such as a #2 Muddler. Use a sinking line and quarter your cast downstream with a classic steelhead presentation.

It gets hot in this canyon; the first time I fished it I thought I'd melt into a little puddle of grease and neoprene. To protect the fish from stress during periods of warm water, this section is closed to angling from mid-June until October 1.

This is fast water, but it gets turbid in low flows.

Frain Ranch. Another good fly fishing section is the 11 miles between Boyle Dam and the California border, the lower part of

you can carry up a hill). Put in at Chiloquin Ridge Rd. bridge (by the power station) and drift through the canyon to the flat water behind the dam near the Chiloquin High School. The pool behind the dam holds bass and other warmwater fish.

The best fishing is in early spring and in fall. Streamer patterns, such as leeches and Woolly Buggers, work well. The techniques and hatches are similar to those on the Williamson.

Upper Deschutes River

The upper Deschutes (above Bend) divides into three sections: source at Little Lava Lake to Crane Prairie Reservoir, Crane Prairie Dam to Wickiup Reservoir, Wickiup Dam to Bend.

In the first section, the Deschutes is a pretty little creek flowing through pine forests and meadows of wildflowers. It's a nice place, but fly fishing is just so-so. The section is only open June 1 to August 31 to protect spawning trout.

The Crane Prairie to Wickiup section is not productive water above FR 42. Below FR 42, however, the river slows, and fishing can be excellent. You can reach this section from the Sheep Bridge campground off FR 4260, or from the bridge on FR 42. Brook trout, browns, and rainbows move up from Wickiup, and some of these fish are quite large. Evening fishing is often good. If a hatch is coming off, by all means match it. Otherwise, tie on a large streamer such as a brown Matuka or an olive Woolly Bugger. Fish it as deep as you can through pools, by undercut banks, across breaks, and along logs. This part of the river is closed after August 31.

Below Wickiup, the Deschutes is a big river whose placid surface conceals its power. Take it seriously. While canoes and small outboards can negotiate much of the river, there are occasional places where it plunges over impassable cataracts. Almost every year someone drowns here due to ignorance and lack of caution. Know where the falls are, and avoid them.

A network of roads (some of them quite rough) gives access to much of the river below Wickiup (see the maps in *Fishing in Oregon* and *Fishing in Oregon's Cascade Lakes*). Fishing for rainbow and brown trout can be good, especially in the evening. The stretch just below Wickiup Dam (accessed from FR 4370) can be a pleasant and productive area.

Below Wickiup, the river holds brown trout and rainbows. Some of the browns are over 15 pounds, but fish that large are seldom taken on flies. There is good spawning habitat in the Spring and Fall rivers, so many of the fish in this stretch are wild.

Middle Deschutes River

This little-fished part of the Deschutes is sandwiched between Bend and Lake Billy Chinook. It is drawn down to a trickle in summer for irrigation. When irrigation ends, flows increase and winter hatches are reliable (for winter hatches, that is). It becomes a good destination or detour between October and April.

Most of the river bank is in private hands, but some good public access points are at Lower Bridge, Odin Falls, Cline Falls, and Tumalo. Winter hatches of note are the ubiquitous blue-winged olive, little black stones, and March browns. The latter usually begin in mid-March, about two weeks later than the hatch starts on many other Oregon rivers.

North Fork of the Middle Fork of the Willamette River

Most people just call it "The North Fork." It's a beautiful, close-to-Eugene tributary that offers fine fly fishing for wild rainbow and cutthroat trout. The river's headwaters are at Waldo Lake.

To reach the North Fork, turn off Hwy. 58 four miles west of Oakridge; you see a sign for "West Fir." Follow the road to West Fir, then take Hwy. 19 out of town. Hwy. 19 (also know as Aufderheide Dr.) parallels the river for much of its fishable length. There are fre-

The North Fork of the Middle Fork of the Willamette has wild trout and is a short drive from Eugene.

quent turn-outs for parking.

This is a small stream, seldom more than 50-feet across. It is bouldery and quick, but has frequent pools and pocket water.

All the fish are native and wild; there's been no stocking since the mid-70s. The river is cold, so the fishing doesn't usually turn on until July. Fish are not huge—11 inches is average—but there are a few that reach 16 inches or more. The river is fly-fishing-only and sees little angling pressure.

Trout in Lakes

Crane Prairie Reservoir

Not far from its headwaters, a dam backs up the Deschutes River to form Crane Prairie Reservoir. But before the dam was built in 1922, there was a Crane Prairie. It was a broad expanse of grass, wildflowers, and stands of pines, through which flowed the Deschutes and several of its tributaries. The streams were filled with large native trout, and pioneer anglers who came here were rewarded with bountiful catches.

The old prairie is now flooded by the waters behind the dam, but the great fishing remains. It is hardly a put-and-take fishery, since the majority of the trout are wild fish that spawn in the Deschutes River.

Crane Prairie is blessed with the best of two worlds: ample sunlight penetrates the shallow water and encourages the growth of fish-nourishing habitat, yet cool inflows from the Deschutes and other creeks keep the temperature at a comfortable level for trout. Although it wasn't planned that way, the habitat is improved by standing snags:

when the dam's floodgates were closed the irrigators didn't bother to log the pines trees.

Crane Prairie has more than fish. It is also one of Oregon's best places to view waterfowl. Osprey, bald eagles, sandhill cranes, herons, and cormorants thrive here.

Access and Facilities

Crane Prairie is 46 miles from Bend via Forest Road 46, or 40 miles via FR 40. Roads skirt the lake, but access is limited. See the map for roads and campgrounds. Cow Camp campground is primitive and has no water; access to the lake is difficult. The other campgrounds are developed and have boat ramps, pit toilets, drinking water, tables, and trash dumpsters. In low water, launching boats from Rock Creek and Quinn River can be difficult.

Bank fishing is non-existent at Crane. Float tube launch points are Rock Creek, Rocky Point, and the end of road 4270-470. The rest of the lake requires a boat.

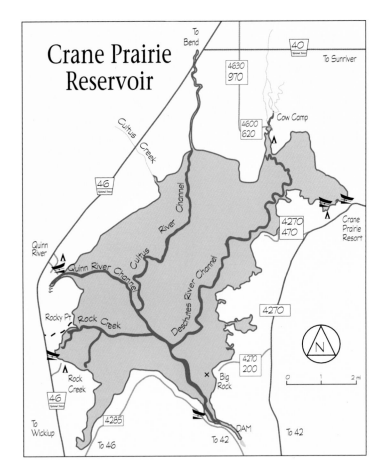

Species

Rainbows (to seven pounds and more) predominate, with some brook trout (to five pounds), whitefish (a state record came from here), and kokanee. While some rainbows are stocked, there is significant natural spawning in the tributaries, and over half the rainbows count as wild fish. Brookies are totally wild, but not native. Largemouth bass, black crappie, bluegills, and sticklebacks were illegally introduced by ecological terrorists masquerading as sportsmen.

When to Fish

The vagaries of spring weather make for variable fishing until June. July can be unbelievable if the damselflies migrate. August can be slow if there's an east wind. September and October can be outstanding.

Services

The resort has boat rentals, limited supplies and tackle, and a good selection of flies. Twin Lakes Resort is nearby and has limited supplies and a restaurant. Both resorts have pay showers and an RV park. The nearest major services are in Bend, Sunriver, and LaPine. There are fly shops in Bend and Sunriver.

Hatches and Other Food

Callibaetis hatch most afternoons from May through September. Dry flies (*e.g.*, Adams) work, but a Flashback Pheasant Tail nymph retrieved slowly on an intermediate line can be a good producer before, during, and after the hatch.

Midges often dominate, especially in morning, evening, and early and late season. A pupa pattern fished just below the surface can work well, and it can also be effective (maybe more so) when very slowly retrieved near the weed tops.

Damselflies. Fish the nymphs from opening day until the end of July. After that, concentrate on other food forms.

Caddis are an often ignored hatch. Try skating an Elk Hair (size 12, brown body) on the

South Sister looms above Crane Prairie.

surface. Soft Hackles can also produce during a hatch; use a repeated lift-then-sink retrieve with the lift as vertical as possible.

Dragonflies and leeches once were dominant foods, but their populations have declined, possibly from weather problems, bass predation, commercial harvest of dragonfly nymphs, or other causes. Leech and dragonfly nymph patterns can still be productive, however. Leeches work well at low light times such as cloudy days, dawn, and dusk.

Other fish. The bigger rainbows are focusing on sticklebacks and baby bass. Try a Woolly Bugger with a strip of flashabou tied along the sides.

Fishing Tips

Long leader. Use a leader that is at least 15 feet long, tapered to 3X. When there is no wind, the lake's pros go as long as 25 feet.

Slow retrieve on an intermediate line. A slow sinking intermediate line is the right choice unless the water is unusually high. The line lets your fly sink down near the weed tops. Retrieve it slowly. If it isn't driving you nuts, your retrieve is too fast. The lake's big trout usually prefer a fly that creeps across the tops of the weeds.

Fish in the channels. In low water years, the fish will concentrate in the channels when the lake warms or drops. You should concentrate there, too. Look for places that are a little deeper than the rest of the bottom.

Don't fish in the channels. In high water years, trout will not concentrate in the channels, but will scatter throughout the lake and be harder to find.

Anchoring. Careful positioning is critical. Too close and you spook the trout, too far off and you can't reach them. Position yourself at least two casts away from the nearest angler. Use two anchors to minimize swing. Be quiet; row or use an electric motor to get in position.

Bank fishing and float tubing. You can't reach any decent water from the bank; you must have a tube or a boat. Best tube launching: Rock Creek area, and the end of road 4270-470.

Time of day. Best fishing is when the wind riffles the water. On most days, this means the half hour just as the sun comes over the mountains, then from 10 a.m. to 5 p.m. Sometimes you can hook a good fish half an hour after sunset, but most of Crane's big trout go to bed at 5 p.m. Overcast days can produce fish all day long.

Seek wind-riffled water. On days with light or variable winds, cast to water that is slightly wind-riffled. Even if you see fish rising in flat, mirror-like water, ignore them and cast where the wind has disturbed the surface. On days of flat calm, fishing will be poor.

Marabou Damsel
(Randall Kaufmann)

Hook:	TMC 200R, sizes 8-12
Thread:	Olive
Tail:	Short olive marabou
Rib:	Copper wire, fine
Body:	Olive marabou. Tie-in butt ends and wrap forward; use fine ends to make wing.
Wing:	Short olive marabou or leftover tips from body wrap. Tear off excess until it's the right length.

The bead head is optional. At Crane Prairie, it is not necessary except in high-water years. Yellow-olive is usually the best color at Crane.

Hosmer Lake

Hosmer has long been a destination for Northwest fly anglers eager to pursue its big brook trout and land-locked Atlantic salmon. Weedy and shallow, it is a fly-fishing-only lake with spectacular mountain vistas, pleasant campgrounds, abundant waterfowl and wildlife . . . and hard to catch fish.

Hosmer lies at the north end of the Cascade Lakes Highway, and vistas are dominated by three mountains: South Sister, Mt. Bachelor, and Broken Top. Nights are cool, and mosquitoes are common near the water's edge. About three miles north of Hosmer Lake, Quinn Creek rises very clear and very cold from springs in the lava rock. Centuries ago, a lava flow dammed the creek and formed Hosmer Lake. It has been steadily filling in with sediment since then, and in a few more centuries it will be a meadow. Until then, it's a great place to go fly fishing, bird watching, and canoeing.

Access and Facilities

Turn at the "Hosmer/E. Elk Lake" sign on FR 46 (34 miles SW of Bend), and follow the signs to Hosmer. There are two campgrounds: South Camp and Mallard Marsh. Both have tables, pit toilets, and trash dumpsters; neither has drinking water.

Bank fishing is impossible due to the marshes and reeds, so you need a watercraft of some kind. Float tubes are popular, as are canoes, rowboats, and other small craft. The only motors allowed are electrics.

South Camp has a paved boat ramp. At Mallard Marsh campground, you can launch a float tube or canoe into a narrow passage that leads to the lake; follow the trail between campsites 14 and 15. These are the only access points.

Species

Land-locked Atlantic salmon average 15 inches, with some over 18. The salmon are beautiful and acrobatic fish. Brook trout to five pounds are also present. There is little natural reproduction of either species. ODFW plans to cease stocking brookies, so their population will decline, and the salmon will dominate the lake.

When to Fish

Fishing is best in spring after the ice melts, and in fall when the weather cools. But this is a great spot, and you should fish it anytime you can get there. This is in a high snow area, so the roads are often blocked from early November to mid-May, or even longer.

Services

Bend and Sunriver have extensive visitor facilities, and there are limited supplies at nearby Elk and Lava Lakes. Lava Lake has pay showers and an RV park. The nearest public phone is at Mt. Bachelor. There are fly shops in Bend, Sunriver, and Sisters. Lava Lake Resort has some flies.

Hatches and Other Food

Callibaetis, midges, water boatmen, crayfish, caddis, leeches, damselflies, and dragonflies. If it wiggles, it lives in Hosmer's rich waters. Mid-day *Callibaetis* hatches are common in summer. Midges are very important, especially at dusk. Some years the fish are eager for adult damselflies in early August.

Fishing Tips

Follow the temperature changes. In the spring, Hosmer's south end warms first, so fish there early in the season. As the season progresses, fish tend to migrate into the channel areas, and even the shallow north end becomes fishable. Few anglers visit the north end, but it's a pretty place, and the fishing can be good; concentrate your casts over the black streaks you see on the bottom, or look for the

Stalcup Adult Damsel
(Shane Stalcup)

Hook:	900BL, sizes 10-12
Thread:	Black
Abdomen:	Braided leader material. Color with Pantone pens (available at art supply stores if your local fly shop doesn't have any).
Wings:	Zing Wing
Thorax:	Poly yarn to match abdomen
Eyes:	Burned monofilament

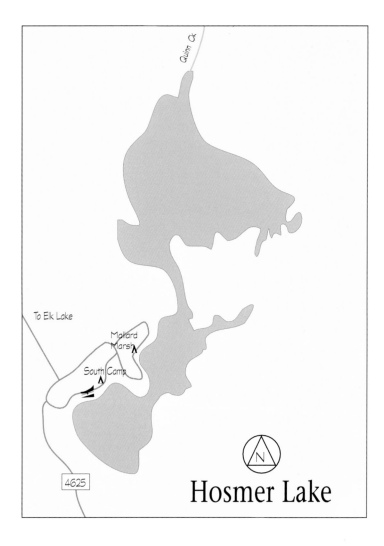

Hosmer Lake

flash of fish feeding subsurface. As the weather cools in fall, the south end is the place to be.

Long thin leaders. Fifteen-foot leaders tapered to 6X. Yup, it's tough.

Work the channel only in low light. In the height of summer, fish concentrate in the narrow channel between Hosmer's north and south ends. They're tempting, highly visible targets. But you're also visible, and you're more scary (to a fish, anyway). Also, there is a lot of canoe traffic. So even if you can see the fish in the channel, save your casts for dawn and dusk or cloudy days.

Use white streamers in the fall. Atlantics are suckers for moving, white flies in the fall. Try a white Woolly Bugger or some other streamer with lots of white and maybe some dark, flashy green with a hint of yellow.

Stealth counts. These fish see a lot of fly anglers. Sneak up on them and make long, careful casts.

Don't ignore the middle. The fish like the weedy areas along the edges of the south end, and most fly anglers are found working these spots. But there are lots of fish, especially Atlantics, in the middle of the lake.

Special Regulations

Fly fishing only with barbless hooks. All Atlantic salmon must be released unharmed. No fishing from a motor-propelled craft when the motor is running. The only allowable motors are electrics.

An angler prepares to release one of Hosmer's land-locked Atlantic salmon.

Mann Lake

I'll bet fewer than a dozen anglers can claim this to be their "local" fishing hole. For the rest of the world, this is a distant and desolate spot. But not unpopular. The fact that you can come to a place this remote and not be lonely gives you some idea how many people are in the world.

There's no reason to come to Mann Lake except to fish, and there's usually plenty of reason to do just that: the lake supports cutthroat trout that often top four pounds. And if you like the desert, this is a great place to be. The sheer eastern face of Steens Mountain rises almost a mile above the lake, and antelope are often seen. Other than that, there's not much to look at except sagebrush and a few cows.

Anglers begin arriving at Mann Lake not long after the ice leaves in spring. It is a good destination for early and late in the season (but don't come in summer). Spring weather can be severe, however. That was the case the first time I visited this lake. I arrived very late at night, as gale-force winds blew snow horizontally. I saw several tents that had been flattened by the wind; people were still in some of them.

Access and Facilities

Mann Lake is on the way to nowhere, unless you count Denio, Nevada as somewhere (few people do). The lake is 100 miles southwest of Burns on the Fields-Denio Rd, a two-lane gravel spur off State Route 78. A large BLM sign marks the turn-off to the lake.

There is camping on the east and west sides. Each camp area has a pit toilet, and the east side has a boat ramp. There are no other facilities. Make sure you bring lots of drinking water.

Chironomid Pupa
(Randall Kaufmann)

Hook:	101 or 900BL, sizes 10-20
Thread:	Black
Tail:	Clear antron
Antennae:	Same as tail
Rib:	White silk thread
Abdomen:	Black turkey biot; keep smooth and slender
Thorax:	Peacock herl
Wing:	Grizzly hen hackle tips

Other body colors: grey, brown, tan. Most midges are matched with size 16-22 hooks. However, at Mann and other desert lakes, there is a spring hatch of large midges that are matched with size 10 and 12 hooks; use a black slender body with white ribbing.

These flies may be presented absolutely still just below the surface film, or be allowed to sink and then be drawn slowly to the surface. Sometimes even a very slow retrieve near the surface can be effective.

The east slope of Steens Mountain rises sharply above Mann Lake.

Species

A hatchery version of the wild Lahontan cutthroat trout are stocked here every other year. They grow to large size (20-inchers are common) and are predacious, beautiful fish, if not especially strong fighters. There is no natural reproduction.

When to Fish

Mann is best known as an early season destination, with anglers arriving immediately after ice-out. Fishing can open up as early as February, but check the ODFW fishing report to be sure there is open water. Fishing drops off as the weather gets hot, then picks up again in September and October.

Services

Burns (100 miles away) is the nearest town. Fields (50 miles south) consists of a combination gas station/mini-mart. If you're not self-contained, don't come to Mann Lake.

Hatches and Other Food

Dragonflies, damselflies, *Callibaetis*, and midges predominate. As with most desert lakes, there is a spring hatch of mega-midges. They are matched by a pupa pattern in size 10 or 12; flies should be thin, with a black body, white ribbing, and a white tuft at the head. Fish them just below the surface, either dead still or with a very slow retrieve.

Because the trout are predators, they respond aggressively to flies that look alive and tasty, so Woolly Buggers and large nymphs are effective.

Fishing Tips

Forget the boat in spring. Early season, fish are found close to shore, often in water hardly over your ankles, so you don't need to go to the middle of the lake. Sometimes a float tube helps a little, but it really isn't necessary. Be stealthy. Wading into the lake until you are thigh or waist deep, then casting back towards shore can be effective.

Watch the midge shucks. Check the water surface for midge shucks to see what size and color to use. You will probably come up with several possibilities. Try them all till you find one that works.

Fall crowds are smaller. 'Nuff said.

Fast retrieves can work. If the fish don't seem to be biting, try a very fast retrieve of a large, dark nymph (eg., size 8 Hare's Ear in dark brown or a Woolly Bugger). The unnaturally fast retrieve seems to stimulate strikes when nothing else works.

Fish often concentrate in pods. I've been here when almost all the fish in the lake seemed to be swimming in a 200 square-foot area. Pay attention to signs of feeding, and if you find one fish, you may have found a few hundred.

Relax at Alvord Hot Springs. This natural hot springs is about 15 miles south of Mann Lake, just off the road. The water is a notch over 100 degrees and slightly sulfurous. It's a great place to ease your casting muscles and watch the desert sky at night.

Special Regulations

Artificial flies and lures only. Two trout per day bag limit, minimum of 16 inches (don't bother; they don't taste good).

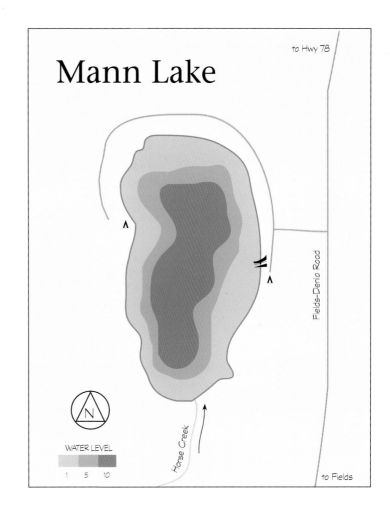

Upper Klamath Lake

Some of the world's largest wild rainbow trout swim here. Fish exceeding ten pounds are not uncommon, and the lake is well-suited to fly fishing.

Upper Klamath Lake is often the largest lake in Oregon. Its size varies depending on snowpack and rainfall. But even if you can cast 80 feet or more, it's a bit daunting to be confronted with almost 100 square miles of water. Further, the fish are highly migratory, and volatile conditions make it hard to come up with a set of rules for finding them.

When you first launch a boat or float tube here, you might feel like a speck of inter-galactic dust. Don't panic! There are lots of fish, and a little knowledge can help narrow the search.

Most of the fly fishing is concentrated in a few areas at the north end. Fish migrate between the lake and its creeks and tributaries, most notably the Williamson and Wood Rivers, which are covered in earlier chapters.

People often get confused out here and wonder about the lake's name. If this is

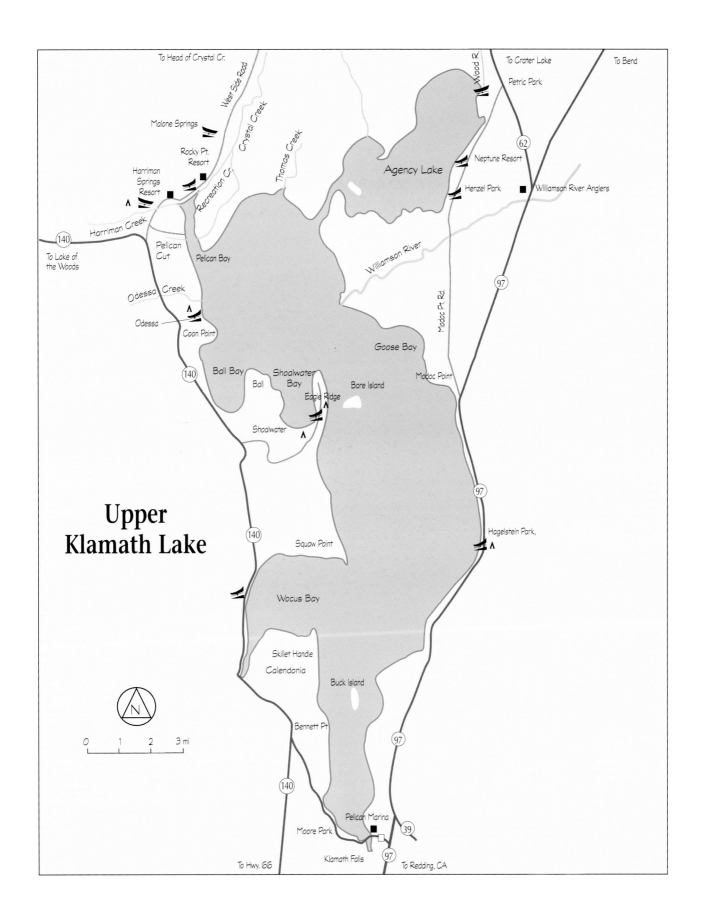

Upper
Klamath Lake

To Head of Crystal Cr.

West Side Road

Malone Springs

Rocky Pt.
Resort

Harriman
Springs
Resort

Crystal Creek

Recreation Cr.

Thomas Creek

140

To Lake of
the Woods

Harriman Creek

Pelican
Cut

Pelican Bay

Odessa Creek

Odessa

Coon Point

140

Ball Bay

Ball

Shoalwater
Bay

Shoalwater

Eagle Ridge

Bare Island

Goose Bay

Modoc Point

Wood R.

To Crater Lake

To Bend

Petric Park

62

Agency Lake

Neptune Resort

Henzel Park

Williamson River Anglers

Williamson River

Madoc Pt. Rd.

97

97

Hagelstein Park,

140

Squaw Point

Wocus Bay

Skillet Handle

Calendonia

Buck Island

Bennett Pt

97

N

0   1   2   3 mi

Pelican Marina

Moore Park

39

97

To Hwy. 66

Klamath Falls

To Redding, CA

Upper Klamath Lake, is there a Lower Klamath Lake? Nope. Just the one lake, but it goes by the double-barreled appellation of Upper Klamath.

Access and Facilities

Hwy 97 skirts the west shore of the lake, but most of the useful fishing access is from Hwy 140, which follows much of the east side. See the map for campgrounds and boat ramps.

Mini Leech
(Randall Kaufmann)

Hook: 200R, sizes 6-14
Thread: To match body/tail color
Tail: Marabou with 3-5 strands of Krystal flash that matches the body color. Tie the marabou on the upper half of hook for the entire length of the shank; this forms an underbody.
Body: Angora goat or Crystal Seal on a dubbing loop.

Tie these in black, rust brown, red, maroon, tan, and olive. Sometimes it makes all the difference in the world to change colors. The bead head is optional, but it's a good idea most of the time. On Upper Klamath Lake, use black, brown, or olive, and skip the bead head.

Normally leeches are slow moving, but they will move quickly when they're pursued. So use several different retrieves until you find one that works well.

Species

Most of the catch is rainbow trout, with fish often going over five pounds, and many over ten. The Klamath strains of rainbows are now being used to stock other lakes because they are resistant to a parasite that lives in many high desert waters. Brook and brown trout are also available.

When to Fish

The lake is open year-round, and a few winter trout are picked up at the south end, near Pelican Marina, but most of the good fishing is between May and October; mid-June to mid-August sees the most pressure, and some of the largest fish. However, the real answer to the question "When is the best time to fish Upper Klamath Lake" is: "It all depends." The trout are highly migratory, and they move often in search of food and better water conditions. It's a good idea to call Rocky Point Resort (541/356-2287) and check on current conditions.

Services

Klamath Falls has extensive visitor facilities, and there are also restaurants and motels in Fort Klamath. Rocky Point Resort on the northwest shore has a restaurant, RV park with full hookups, and rooms and cabins to rent. The resort also rents boats and canoes, and has some fishing tackle and flies.

Hatches and Other Food

While the usual fare of dragonfly and damselfly nymphs, caddis, and *Callibaetis* are present, leeches and forage fish make up most of the diet from ice-out to late June. The lake is rich in tui chub (roach), blue chub, fathead minnows, sculpins, and even lamprey eels.

Fishing Tips

Temperature and alkalinity drive fish behavior. Because this is a shallow lake in a sunny area, the water warms quickly in summer. With increases in temperature and alkalinity (and corresponding decreases in oxygen), trout cruise the lake in search of better conditions.

This makes the fishing unpredictable. You might fish here in June and hit the jackpot with ten and fifteen-pound rainbows. The next year—or next week—you might fish the same spot in the same way and get skunked.

Most of the year, stay north. Water conditions are such that it is rarely useful to fish south of Eagle Ridge after mid-June.

Pelican Bay stays algae-free. Conditions in Pelican Bay are radically different than in the rest of the lake. As the season warms, the main lake becomes thick with algae. Pelican Bay gets weedy in the channel leading to the main lake, but it has several cool creeks and springs. Their inflows keep the bay clear of algae blooms, and trout tend to concentrate there as the lake heats up.

Pelican Bay best for tubers. Pelican Bay offers the best access and water conditions for float tubers.

Every creek and spring creates a mini-environment. The water flowing from each creek or spring has a different temperature. Some inlet creeks may run at 75 degrees, while less than a mile away a different creek might have water 20 degrees cooler. A trout's response to these conditions will vary depending on conditions in the rest of the lake.

Migratory trout head for the rivers. By late June, a few trout head towards rivers and creeks, such as the Williamson and Wood rivers. As the season progresses, more and more fish swim to the cooler, more oxygenated waters of the streams that feed the lake. This means that fishing near the mouths of the rivers and creeks gets better as the season progresses. By the first fall frost, trout head for the rivers in large numbers, searching for better water and a place to spawn.

Predatory fish. You don't grow ten- and 15-pound trout on a diet of size 22 midges.

Pelicans are a common sight on Upper Klamath Lake.

These fish like juicy meals such as leeches, dragonfly and damselfly nymphs, and other fish. Flies that imitate these food forms do well, with black and dark brown the best colors; olive is productive only in clear water. Woolly Buggers and Denny Rickard's Seal Buggers are good pattern choices. Zonkers in white or with some yellow also work well because they imitate baitfish.

Intermediate line. The best fishing is subsurface, so a floating line is of very limited utility here. On the other hand, most sinking-tip lines and faster sinking lines drop too quickly. Therefore an intermediate line is the best choice, except perhaps on sunny, calm days in clear water; then a clear line, such as the Scientific Anglers Stillwater line, is a good choice if the water is deep enough.

Leaders. Use a 10-12 foot leader tapered to 3X or 4X in algae-tinted water, and a 12-15 foot leader in clear water.

Watch for signs of stress. The variable water conditions can leave the fish in a stressed state. If you catch a few fish that seem sluggish for their size, either move to a better place or stop fishing altogether.

Special Regulations

Bag limit: one trout per day.

Davis Lake

As lakes go, Davis Lake is a mere youngster. It was formed about 3,000 years back, when a lava flow blocked Odell Creek's path to the Deschutes River. A large, shallow lake was formed, and fish thrive in it.

The creek offers spawning habitat, and the lake supplies abundant food. As a result, Davis Lake supports wild rainbow trout that grow to five pounds or more.

With conditions like this, it didn't take long for anglers to discover Davis Lake. One of the first things they discovered was that it was too weedy to troll in, and too shallow for bait fishing. So there were few complaints when the lake was designated as fly-fishing-only in the 1930s. It has remained that way ever since.

This is a big lake (over 5,000 acres), and many first-time visitors feel intimidated by its size. But finding fish is easier than it might first appear. Fish tend to concentrate in three areas, so despite its size Davis Lake has a surprising intimacy.

With so much to offer, Davis Lake has long been a popular destination for Northwest fly anglers. Not only does it grow large trout, but it has three very pleasant campgrounds and nice views of Cascade peaks.

Recently, however, the lake fell on hard times. A string of dry winters left Davis Lake in a pitiful state. Most of the water was gone, and the few remaining fish were stressed by high water temperatures. But after a few wet winters, the lake was overflowing, and fish are now doing well. Davis Lake's many friends hope it continues to get the water it needs.

Access and Facilities

Davis Lake is near the southern end of FR 46, the Cascade Lakes Highway. East and West Davis campgrounds are just across Odell

Creek from each other, but are reached from separate roads. Lava Camp, at the lake's north end, is closed most of the year to protect nesting bald eagles. Each of these three campgrounds has a boat ramp; only Lava Camp's is paved. There is a rough campground at Ranger Creek, off FR 4660.

When the water is not high, the lake can be fished from shore near Odell Creek, but usually you need a boat or float tube. Tubers can easily launch at East or West Davis. Ambitious tubers can park a car at the gate that blocks the road to Lava Camp and walk a mile down the road, then launch at the campground and fish the lava dam area.

Species

Rainbow trout are the quarry at Davis Lake. Odell Creek is good spawning habitat, and most of the trout are wild fish. A few rainbows of the Klamath strain are stocked as fingerlings. Hatchery fish have their adipose fin clipped.

Tui chub (roach) are present in the lake, as are illegally-stocked largemouth bass. There is no limit on the bass, so kill 'em if you catch 'em.

When to Fish

Davis is open all year, but snow blocks access until spring and closes it in fall. May to October, fishing can be excellent, with the usual slow-down during the dog days of August.

Services

Crescent Junction on Hwy 58 has some services, including motels, stores, and cafes. South Twin and Crane Prairie resorts have showers, ice, and limited supplies. South Twin rents cabins and has a restaurant.

There are fly shops in Bend and Sunriver. Limited supplies and flies are available at Crane Prairie, Twin Lakes, and Lava Lake resorts.

Hatches and Other Food

I fished the Odell channel at dusk one evening and recorded these species of trout food: *Callibaetis* spinner fall, *Caenis* mayfly

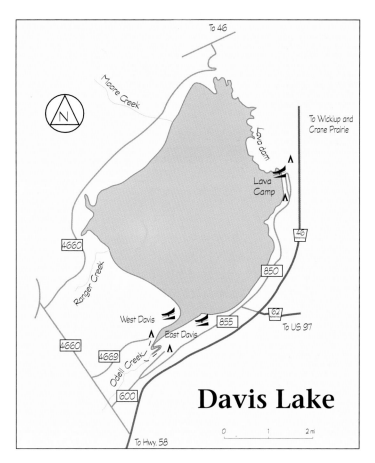

hatch, caddis hatch, two kinds of midges, and a daphnia bloom. Besides the insects I encountered that evening, dragonflies, damselflies, leeches, crayfish, and chub all provide food. Davis has legendary *Callibaetis* and midge hatches.

Fishing Tips

Best places to fish. It's a big lake, but fish usually concentrate at the lava dam, the west shore between Ranger and Moore creeks, and the Odell Creek channel.

Watch the water temperature. Temperature varies greatly throughout the lake due to the influence of tributary creeks and springs. Carry a streamside thermometer, and measure the water temperature. If it's over 72 or 74, find a different spot to fish. The lava dam area is the warmest, so it is good in spring, poor in July and August. In early fall, fish tend to concentrate in the Odell channel to find cooler water.

Wind is everything. When there is no wind

Chan's Chironomid Pupa
(Brian Chan)

Hook: 2457, sizes 16-22
Thread: Black
Tail: White poly yarn
Ribbing: Fine silver tinsel
Body: Black thread
Wingcase: Pheasant tail fibers
Thorax: Peacock herl

and it's sunny, fishing will be the pits. Seek wind-riffled water, if you can find it.

These fish are selective. The big trout can be incredibly fussy about patterns. When they want something, it needs to match the size, color, stage, and action of the natural insect.

Go no-hackle for Callibaetis duns. In general, dry flies on a lake work better with little or no hackle.

Cripples and emergers. Flies that imitate emerging or crippled insects often work well during a hatch, especially during a midge hatch.

Special Regulations

Fly-fishing only with barbless hooks. No limit on size or number of warmwater species.

A great blue heron greets the dawn on Davis Lake.

East Lake

The volcanic heritage of East Lake is readily apparent. Formations of twisted rock, a huge slide of white pumice, and giant cracks in solid basalt all point to a violent—and rather recent— past. When you fish in the maw of this volcano, you feel you are connected to the center of the earth.

The center of the earth may be where you feel you are going to end up when you connect with one of East Lake's mammoth brown trout or outsized rainbows. When a fish bores into the depths, and your rod bends in a deep arc that reaches into the water, you may wonder where it will all end.

Of course not all the lake's fish are monsters. Many are fiesty 12-inch landlocked Atlantic salmon. That's one of the things I like best about East Lake: I never know what's going to grab my fly. It could be a foot-long Atlantic, a 14-inch brook trout, a 20-inch rainbow, or a ten-pound brown trout.

East Lake is naturally barren, so all these fish are stocked. The salmon, brookies, and smaller rainbows feed on midges and *Callibaetis*, and the big rainbows and brown

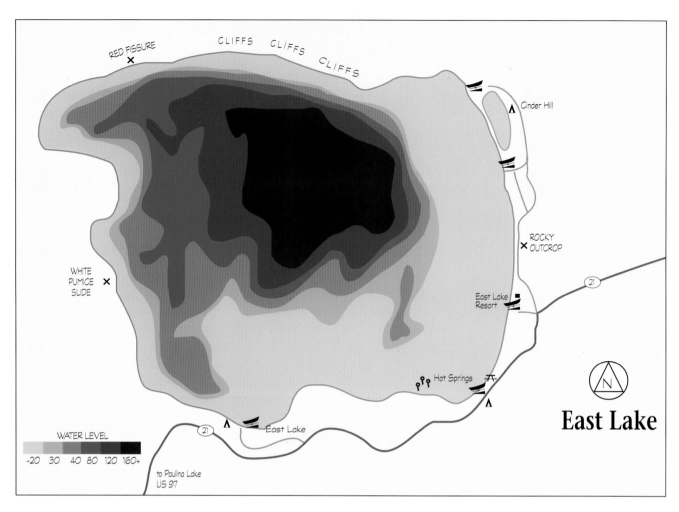

trout feed on all the other fish. The lake also has tui chub, so there is lots of fodder for the bigger trout.

When you come to East Lake, dress for cold weather; it's a high, harsh climate, and I've never been too warm here. Also, this area is prime black bear habitat, and the big furry guys are frequent midnight visitors to campground dumpsters. So if you camp here, put your food and cooking gear inside the car, and don't put a slab of bacon under your pillow if you sleep in a tent.

Access and Facilities

From Hwy 97, 22 miles south of Bend (six miles north of La Pine), take FR 21. East Lake is 17 miles distant. There are three large campgrounds, but I feel the East Lake Campground (the first one you come to) is best for fly fishers, especially those with float tubes.

You can walk the shoreline between the rocky point east of East Lake Campground and the large cove in the lake's northwest corner. Much of this is fishy water that can be reached from shore. An ambitious angler could carry a float tube along the shore, then launch and fish from the tube.

Species

East Lake supports brook, rainbow, and brown trout, and landlocked Atlantic salmon. The brookies and rainbows average 12-14 inches, but the rainbows can go over 20 inches. Brook trout are no longer stocked, and the population is declining. There are many brown trout that go well over ten pounds, but they're hard to catch. Rainbows, salmon, and brown trout are all stocked fish. Tui chub (roach) are also present and are forage for larger fish. Kokanee are stocked, but dwell too deep for fly anglers.

When to Fish

The road is seldom open before late May, and closes in early fall. If you can get here, fishing is usually good.

Services

East Lake Resort has boat rentals, cabins, an RV park, a cafe, and a small store with very limited fly tackle. Restaurants, motels, and other services are available in La Pine, and anything you could possibly want can be found in Bend or Sunriver. The nearest fly shops are in Bend and Sunriver.

Hatches and Other Food

Callibaetis and midges can be plentiful, but other hatches are limited. The big browns feed primarily on other fish.

Fishing Tips

Browns like "cover." Brown trout are cautious and predatory. They like rocky structure because it offers protection and opportunities to ambush baitfish. Other forms of "cover" are depth, darkness, and wave action.

Fish windward shores. The first thing I do at East Lake is check the wind direction. Then I fish the shore the wind is blowing *against*.

Margins are best. There are extensive weed beds in the shallow areas in front of the resort; fish just west of them. The area in front of East Lake Campground has rocky structure, shallow areas, and other fish attractions; it can be easily fished from a float tube launched at the campground. The margins around the west shore often produce well. The hot springs are usually good just after ice-out because the water is warmer. The biggest mistake anglers make at East Lake is fishing water that is too deep.

Clear water means tough choices. You need a thin tippet in the clear water, but if you want to hang onto a big brown you need strength. There is no "right" answer to this problem.

Watch the weather. The wind can blow hard up here, and the lake can quickly go from placid to white caps. Thunder storms are not uncommon. Keep a weather eye out, and be safe.

Be prepared for anything. One of the pleasures of East Lake is that you never know what's going to hit your fly, from a ten-inch Atlantic salmon to a ten-pound brown trout.

Atlantics like white moving flies in fall. From September to season's end, Atlantic salmon are suckers for a moving white streamer.

Special Regulations

There is a mercury advisory for East Lake. Don't eat any fish until you have read the warnings in the angling regulations.

Bunny Leech

Hook: 5263 or 300, sizes 2-8

Thread: To match body

Tail: Thin strip of straight-cut rabbit, on the skin

Body: Thin strip of cross-cut rabbit. Wrap around hook shank from back to front. Tie in a few strands of Krystal Flash at the head

I think this is too fat to look like a leech, but fish (especially brown trout) love it, and that's the only opinion that counts. Besides, it's an easy tie. Good body colors are black, rust-brown, olive, maroon, purple, and white. A bead head or weight under the body can be added.

Chickahominy Reservoir

Chickahominy is not a lake that will win any beauty contests. It squats in a hollow in the sage brush plains west of Burns. It's muddy, it's in the middle of nowhere, and there's nothing to look at but sagebrush. I don't know why anyone would go here—except for the large, fat trout.

Like many desert lakes in the Northwest, Chickahominy is moderately alkaline and gets lots of sunshine. That's a recipe for growing a bumper crop of the kind of food that makes trout big and fat.

But not always. While Chickahominy usually has some four and five pound rainbows cruising around, sometimes it has no fish at all. Sometimes the whole lake isn't there. That's because the reservoir is an odd watershed: it has no true inlet. All the water trickles in from melting snow. So in years when the Ochoco National Forest sees little snow, the reservoir shrinks under the summer sun. And sometimes it shrivels into nothing but caked mud. At other times, the desert heat can cause so much algae to bloom that the oxygen is sucked from the lake, and the fish die.

When there is water and fish, however, Chickahominy's assets outweigh its liabilities. Then large, hefty rainbows will grab your Woolly Bugger or a midge pupa, and suddenly this becomes the most beautiful place on earth.

Access and Facilities

Chickahominy is just off Hwy. 20 near Riley, a few miles west of Burns. There is a sign on the highway, and a short gravel road leads to the lake. There isn't much here: a paved boat ramp, some outhouses, some wind-sheltered picnic tables. Camp wherever you want.

Rutted dirt roads go part way along each side of Chickahominy. If your vehicle doesn't have a lot of ground clearance, stay off these roads. When they're wet, even a four-wheel drive truck can get stuck.

Species

Rainbow trout are stocked as fingerlings and grow to 10-12 inches by the following spring. If left in the lake another year, they'll reach 18 inches, and a year later they'll push four pounds.

When to Fish

Chickahominy is a good early season destination. The lake can open up as early as February, and while fishing can be unpleasant due to wind and cold, it can be good. March through early May can be excellent. You don't want to be here in July or August. Fishing improves again with cooler temperatures in fall, but check the water level first.

Services

Riley sports a gas station/cafe/store. Burns has motels, restaurants, and a tackle store

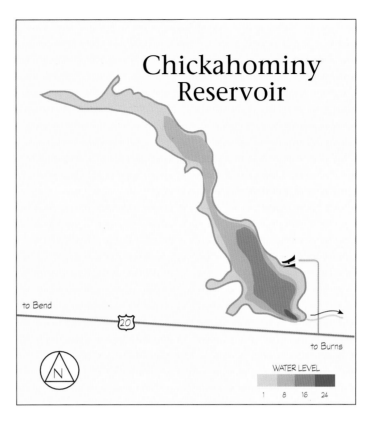

with some fly gear. The nearest fly shops are in Bend, but it's a long trek from here to there.

Hatches and Other Food

Dragonflies, scuds, *Callibaetis,* and midges dominate the trout diet. Dragonfly nymph patterns fished over the weed beds are productive, especially early in the season. *Callibaetis* hatches are common beginning in May. Because many of the fish are large, big Woolly Buggers and leech patterns are effective.

Fishing Tips

Fish are often reachable from shore. A boat or float tube can be useful, but is not necessary. The lake's coves and fingers mean many fish can be easily reached from shore.

Rainbows hang around the south end in spring. The only gravel in the lake is near the south end (boat ramp area). The rainbows head there in an effort to spawn.

Expect murky water. The constant desert wind stirs up the lake and makes the water turbid,

Woolly Bugger

Hook:	5263, sizes 2-10
Thread:	To match body
Tail:	Marabou that matches the body. Add 3-5 strands of Krystal Flash
Rib:	Gold, silver, or copper wire
Body:	Chenille or chenille plus rabbit
Hackle:	Palmered black saddle hackle, or color to match body

You should have lots of these in your box, with a mix of colors and sizes. Good body colors include black, green-olive, yellow-olive, brown, maroon, purple, and white. A bead head can be added, or weight under the body. In lakes where trout grow large and feed on other fish, try putting a strip of flashabou down each side.

so you can get away with a 3X or 2X tippet and a flashier fly than you might usually use.

Don't be a slob. Since the only outhouses are near the boat ramp, you need to understand personal hygiene when you are at other parts of the lake. It's okay to pee on the sagebrush, but when it's time for number two, dig an eight-inch deep hole; don't just squat and leave it on the ground like so many people seem to do here.

You can park on Hwy. 20, then negotiate the fence and walk to the lake's northern reaches. This is useful if you have a car that doesn't belong on deeply-rutted dirt roads.

Make sure there are fish in the lake. In past years, Chickahominy has dried up a couple of times. Even when there is water, there are periodic fish kills due to heavy algae blooms that suck all the oxygen out of the lake. So check with ODFW before you go; make sure the lake is still alive.

Not the most scenic lake in Oregon, Chickahominy lies in a depression in a sage brush plain.

High Lakes

For many anglers, a hike through the mountains to a secluded lake ringed with trees and boulders is a special treat. Oregon is blessed with many such opportunities: the Coast Range, the Cascades, the Wallowas, the Strawberry Wilderness, the Blue Mountains—no matter where you are in the state, there are mountains and mountain lakes nearby.

Some of these lakes have self-sustaining populations of fish, but most are stocked by ODFW with rainbow, brook, and cutthroat trout. Most lakes are stocked with only one species, and usually only every other year. Deeper lakes will allow trout to winter over and grow larger, but other lakes may suffer a heavy winter kill if the lake freezes too deep.

Most fish in the high lakes average 8-12 inches. Some lakes may support fish up to 15 inches, or even a bit bigger. But big fish are not the reason most anglers come to the mountains. They come for a unique experience, to find solitude and refreshment, and to get a different perspective on the world. When you think about it, those are trophies worth pursuing.

Choosing a Lake

Fishing in Oregon lists all the fishable lakes in Oregon, so that is a good place to start. However, *Fishing in Oregon* is updated only every five years, and since the high lakes are at the mercy of winter weather, things can change radically in just a year. Therefore it is often a good idea to check before heading into the hills in search of fish. If a lake is in a

A high lakes rainbow is unhooked to fight again.

national forest, the local ranger station may have current information. Otherwise, check with the nearest ODFW office.

One good strategy for fishing the high lakes is to go to a lake basin. Often there are areas where many lakes are close to each other. This gives you the opportunity to set up a base camp, then sample several different lakes. Some popular lake basins include Mink Lake in the central Cascades, the Sky Lakes Wilderness in the southern Cascades, and the Lakes Basin in the Wallowas.

If you are not an experienced hiker, beware of overestimating your abilities. Start with simple one-day trips of three miles or less. You will learn your limits and have a safer, more satisfying experience.

Not all the high lakes require a strenuous hike. Some are within a mile or two of a paved road, and others can be reached by dirt or gravel roads.

Wilderness Areas

Many of the high lakes are in Wilderness Areas. When you enter a Wilderness Area, you must have a wilderness permit. These are available at self-service stands at trailheads and wilderness boundaries. Also, Wilderness Areas have their own set of rules. These usually include:

Don't camp or build a fire within 100 feet of a lake, stream, or trail.

Don't use mechanized equipment, including mountain bikes.

Don't camp in areas posted for rehabilitation.

Don't cut or damage live trees or shrubs.

In addition, there may be specific rules for certain areas. For example, some of the more popular places have prohibitions against campfires within a large area.

When to Fish

Many lakes above 6,000 feet are not ice-free until early July (especially in the northern half of Oregon). The first thing that happens when the snow and ice melt is that mosquitoes hatch out of the damp soil in unbelievable numbers and search eagerly for something warmblooded . . . like you. It takes a month before they are reduced to bearable numbers. And even in the best of times, they can make life unpleasant for the unprepared. Bring lots of bug sauce; after you put it on, be sure to wash your hands thoroughly because DEET—the active ingredient in most repellents—repels fish as well as mosquitoes.

Mountain weather is always iffy, and by October it can be dangerously so. Thus, between the bugs and the onset of winter, most mountain fishing takes place between mid-July and mid-October. And the higher you go, the shorter the window of opportunity.

What to Take

The first rule about walking into the mountains is: Take it seriously. I'm a firm believer in the "ten essentials," items you should always have with you on a hike. They are:
Map
Compass (know how to use it)
Raingear and extra clothes in case of bad weather
First aid kit
Knife
Matches in waterproof case (or lighter)
Fire starter, such as a candle or chemical starter
Emergency food
Flashlight
Sunscreen

Fishing Tips

While most of the same fishing guidelines apply to the high lakes as to other lakes, there are a few differences. Here are some of them.

Flies to carry. Some good fly patterns to carry are: Adams (sizes 14-18), Elk Hair Caddis (tan or dark brown body, sizes 14-18), Pheasant Tail Nymph or Gold Ribbed Hares Ear (sizes 12-18), Griffiths Gnat (size 20), Flying Ant (sizes 12-14), Olive Woolly Bugger (sizes 8-10).

Hungry fish. Most high lakes don't have a lot of natural food. Therefore, the trout tend to be more opportunistic and less selective about fly patterns. That doesn't mean they'll take anything you throw out there, just that they are more flexible than their lowland cousins.

The exception. The exception to the above tip is midge hatches, which are especially common at dusk. Midges are about the only insect that hatches in volume in the mountain lakes, and large quantities of same size/same color insects is a major cause of selective trout. If you use a midge pupa, you should be pretty close to the size and color of the natural.

A solution to the exception. On the other hand, the trout seem to be un-selective about a dry midge pattern. I do much better with a Griffiths Gnat at high altitudes than I do in the flatlands. I don't know why, but the

Black Flying Ant

Hook:	900BL, sizes 12-20
Thread:	Black
Abdomen:	Black deer overtopping black antron
Wing:	Dark blue dun hackle tips, tied delta style
Hackle:	Brown or black furnace, tied in center
Thorax:	Black antron to match abdomen

Sizes 12 and 14 are most useful. Brown or rust-brown are also effective colors.

higher you go the more receptive trout are to a Griffiths Gnat. I only carry one color (standard peacock herl body) and one size (#20).

Ants. There are a lot of carpenter ants in the mountains. These winged creatures are often blown out of the trees and onto the lakes. Always have a few ant patterns in your fly box. Fish them like a dry fly.

Gold Lake

This fly-fishing-only lake offers wild brookies and rainbows up to 18 inches, with an average size around 12 inches. An easy drive for Eugene-area anglers, Gold Lake is just off Hwy 58. Look for a sign a couple of miles west of the summit. A two-mile gravel road leads to the lake. The road is usually snow-free by late May. A small campground offers sites on both sides of the outlet creek. There is a paved boat ramp near the bridge.

Gold Lake covers about 100 acres and reaches a maximum depth of 40 feet. Rainbow trout must be released, but brookies are so numerous that ODFW has removed the bag limit and would appreciate it

Gold Lake, a fly-fishing-only water, is a short drive from Eugene.

if you'd fry up a bunch of them for dinner.

Bank fishing opportunities are quite limited, so a float tube or small boat is a big advantage. Motors are not allowed. A trail heads into the forest at the end of the east-side camping area. From it you can find tube launching sites or wade in and fish afoot. There is a rough trail on the west side, but it is not useful to anglers.

Fishing is good throughout the lake, not just on the margins. I feel the northeast half offers better fishing. Use a long leader with a thin tippet (15 feet, 5X is preferred). Hatches include midges, caddis, *Callibaetis*, dragonflies, and damselflies.

Gold Lake is a good base camp for reaching other mountain lakes, such as Island Lake and the Marilyn Lakes. Lower Marilyn Lake is only a 20-minute walk from Gold Lake, even if you're carrying a float tube. It's peaceful and tree-lined, and has a nice view of Diamond Peak. The fish are smaller than at Gold Lake, but it's a nice spot

Delintment Lake

If you don't live in Burns, Delintment is probably not a destination lake. But if you are traveling through the region or are fishing Chickahominy and want a change of pace, make a detour to this delightful little lake in the Ochoco National Forest. At 50 acres, Delintment's a perfect size for float tubers. You can also find good spots for bank fishing.

Rainbow trout are stocked every year, and it is a put-and-take fishery. While Delintment's trout are winter-killed most years, every few years the weather will be mild enough to let them live another year. Then you'll find trout averaging 15 inches, with a few up to 20, and they will readily take a fly.

From Hwy. 20 a few miles east of Riley, take Silver Creek Rd., then follow FR 45 to Delintment. There is a pleasant campground amid mature ponderosa pines, and a boat ramp. The road can be snow-blocked well into spring.

The entire lake offers good fishing, but the margins and coves are best. The dam end is deepest, but nearly all of the lake's water can be fished by a well-equipped fly angler. Don't take the fish for granted; they need a well-presented fly on a thin tippet (4X or less). Fishing is best early in the season

Laurence Lake

Laurence Lake is an irrigation impoundment in the Hood River Valley. Rainbows are stocked, but there are also significant populations of wild spawning rainbows and cutthroat that often reach 15 inches. Only finclipped rainbows can be kept, and only artificial flies and lures (no bait) are permitted. There is limited but pleasant camping.

To reach Laurence, take Hwy. 35 from Hood River and turn off for Parkdale. Once in Parkdale, turn south on Clear Creek Rd. and go three miles to Laurence Lake Rd. The lake is four miles down this road. A gravel road skirts the east side of the lake, but it is blocked half way. You can carry a float tube down the blocked portion and find a good launch point near the inlet creek.

The north end offers the best fishing for wild trout. The usual hatches happen, and the standard fly patterns work well.

Laurence Lake contains a fragile population of wild native bull trout, a fish that may soon receive an Endangered Species Listing throughout Oregon. If this happens, Laurence Lake may be closed to protect bull trout. In the mean time, you should not target bull trout in Laurence Lake, and if you happen to hook one by accident, take special care to release it unharmed.

Lost Lake (Mt. Hood)

This large, deep lake has three attractions for fly anglers: a spectacular view of Mt. Hood, brown trout that reach 18 inches or more, and a hatch of yellow mayflies the size of Buicks. In addition to the browns there are rainbow trout that average 10-12 inches, with an occasional five-pound lunker to keep you alert. The rainbows are stocked, but the browns are wild.

To reach Lost Lake from Portland, turn onto E. Lolo Pass Rd. at Zig Zag, and go 26 miles on mostly paved roads; follow the signs carefully for Lost Lake, *not* Lost Creek. This is the shortest route for Portland-area anglers. From Hood River, drive to Dee and take Lost Lake Rd.

The lake hosts a large campground set among fir trees, bear grass, and wild rhodo-

Timberline Emerger
(Randall Kaufmann)

Hook:	3721 or 200R, sizes 12-16
Thread:	Gray
Tail:	Gray marabou kept short and thick
Rib:	Copper wire
Abdomen:	Gray Partridge SLF or angora goat mixed with Haretron
Legs:	Brown neck hackle
Wing:	Grizzly hen tips. Tie them in a "V," with the feathers curving away from each other, on top of the fly.

This is a good searching pattern for high lakes. It is generic enough to look like lots of kinds of food, especially if you're a hungry trout that's never sure were it's next meal is coming from. Gray, tan, and olive are good colors. Keep it sparse.

Use a floating line. After casting to a likely-looking spot, let this fly slowly sink a few feet, then slowly retrieve it until it nears the surface. Then let it sink again, and repeat.

Lost Lake, near the summit of Santiam Pass, offers excellent fly fishing for trout up to 20 inches.

northeast corner is near the boat ramp at the store. The west corner is about a mile from where the road ends near the store. A trail goes around the lakeshore.

Although the resort rents boats, they want them back before the hatch really starts, so bring your own watercraft. Also, mosquitoes can be fierce.

Lost Lake (Santiam Pass)

There are several Lost Lakes in Oregon. This one is near the summit of Santiam Pass (Hwy. 22). For awhile, landlocked Atlantic salmon were stocked here, but the experiment was terminated a few years ago. Today the catch is rainbow trout that are stocked as fingerlings and a self-sustaining population of brook trout. Despite its high altitude, Lost Lake does not have a winter-kill problem. This, combined with the catch-and-release regulations, means Lost Lake's trout have a chance to grow, and many reach 15 inches, with a few approaching 20.

Turn off Highway 22 near mile post 77; the lake is visible from the road. A gravel/dirt road leads to the lake and gives access to the west and south shores. There is a simple campground with outhouses here.

While a lot of fish can be reached by wading from shore, a float tube is a real advantage. Fish can often be spotted, but they can see you, too, so be stealthy. An intermediate line and a floating line are both useful. Be careful with the intermediate: it's easy to let it sink below the level of cruising trout.

Fishing in this lake is very dependent on water conditions. A lack of winter snow or spring rain can cause Lost Lake to shrink. When it gets too small, find another place to fish.

dendrons. There is also a resort with cabins, store, and boat rentals. A paved boat ramp is located near the store.

The "hex" hatch (*Hexagenia limbata*) is what most excites fly fishers here. It begins in early July and continues for a couple of weeks. Hot weather in June and early July intensifies the hatch; without hot weather it will sputter. Starting at sunset, big nymphs rise off the bottom and emerge on the surface, where many are taken by trout. You can do well with either a big yellow dry fly (Paradrake-style) or a large (size 4 or so) light brown nymph fished near the bottom on a long leader with a split shot. The dry is more fun. Fishing can be good until the legal limit of one hour past sunset, so bring a flashlight.

Lost Lake is roughly triangular, and the best fishing is in the corners within 100 feet or so of shore. You can reach these areas with a float tube and a little shoe leather. The southeast corner is near the Organization Camp; park in the lot and walk to shore. The

Steelhead

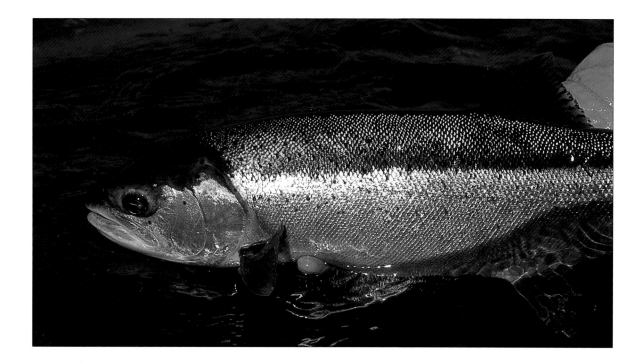

Steelhead Tips

This chapter summarizes a few bread-and-butter steelheading techniques and lists several tips. There are many ways to catch steelhead, some of which are a bit bizarre. I've only included the most straightforward.

Finding Good Water

If you're not on good water, it doesn't matter how well you cast and present your fly; you can't catch fish that aren't there. The primary factors that determine where steelhead lie are the speed of the current and the depth of the water. Most of the time you will find catchable summer steelhead where the water is three to six feet deep with a current that moves about as fast as you would normally walk. While depth and speed are most important, boulders and other structure can make a run even more attractive to steelhead.

Some good places to look for steelhead are:

Below a riffle or point of land. Fish lie in the transition from the fast water formed by the riffle to the slower water near shore.

Below breaks, where the river deepens and slows.

Alongside, in front of, and behind large rocks.

Alongside ledges.

In slowish water that is near faster water, or (better) in slow water between lanes of fast current.

Places where the bottom forms a slot or trench.

Poor places to look for steelhead are sudden transitions where very slow water is adjacent to very fast water, backeddies, very slow or stagnant water, and very fast water.

Classic Wet Fly Presentation

The classic steelhead presentation is a wet-fly swing. Position yourself at the head of a run, and cast down-and-across river at a 45-degree angle. Immediately mend line (usually upstream), so the fly slowly swings across the river with your line as straight as possible. While the fly is swinging do nothing. Don't wiggle the rod, mend line, strip line;

do *nothing*. When the fly reaches the end of its swing, step downstream two or three feet and cast again. And again, and again. Step-cast-swing until the end of the run.

For most summer fish, a seven- or eight-weight rod is best, with a floating line and a nine-foot leader tapered to 1X. Some steelheaders prefer a double-taper line; while it doesn't overhead cast as far as a weight-forward line, it roll casts better, which is an advantage when backcast room is limited.

Fishing Deep

In cold water a steelhead is less likely to move very far to intercept a fly. Therefore the classic presentation works best when the water temperature is above 52-54 degrees. Below that, steelhead tend to stay near the bottom, where the classic presentation with a traditional steelhead fly probably won't reach them.

There are several ways to reach a bottom-hugging steelhead in cold water. One is to use a sink-tip line. Another is with a heavily-weighted fly. Sometimes it takes both. When using a sink-tip, shorten your leader to about four feet. You can continue using the step-cast-swing presentation, but now your fly will be closer to the steelhead's level.

Deep Dead Drift Presentation

Another method of fishing deep uses a weighted fly and an indicator (warning: some traditionalists turn up their noses at this method). Use a floating line with four feet of 0X or 1X leader (a straight leader is fine; it doesn't need to be tapered). Tie a two-inch length of thick poly yarn to the end of the leader; use an improved clinch knot around the middle of the yarn.

Just above the yarn indicator, tie a length of straight (untapered) leader material directly to the other leader; use an improved clinch knot. This new leader should be slightly shorter than the depth of the run you are going to fish. Use the thinnest leader you can get away with, usually 1X-3X, so the fly will sink faster and have less drag. Your leader system now forms a right angle with the indicator at the corner; this helps the fly

sink faster and drift more naturally. Dress the indicator heavily with floatant and tie on a weighted fly, such as the Big Bird.

Cast into slots, troughs, along rocks and ledges, and anywhere you think steelhead might be lying. Treat the indicator like a dry fly: mend so it will drift without drag, and manage your loose line so you can strike quickly when the indicator goes underwater. It will take awhile for the fly to sink to the bottom, so cast ahead of the fish.

This technique works especially well when used from a drifting boat, but it is also effective when bank fishing. Anytime you have pocket water, ledges, or steelhead which are ingesting insect larvae or salmon roe, this is the best fly fishing tactic. The Upper Rogue, many coastal rivers, and most small creeks are ideally suited to this technique.

Unfortunately, this rig is a pain to cast because the indicator has so much air resistance. A different indicator, such as a small Corkie, casts better, but I feel the yarn system catches more fish because it is more sensitive to a subtle take.

Tips

Stand to one side of the run. A common mistake is to stand *in* the run that is being fished. Usually it is better to stand at the edge or a couple of feet to one side.

Choosing a run for low light. Under summer water conditions, steelhead respond best to a fly when sunlight is not on the water. That's why most steelhead fishing is done in the morning and in the evening. When choosing a run in a canyon, smart anglers pick the side of the river that has shade the longest. For example, when fishing the Deschutes, the east bank will be shaded longer in the morning than the west bank. In the evening, water near the west bank will be shaded longer.

Exceptions to the above. When the water temperature is low, say under 45 degrees, the amount of sunlight is not a major factor. In fact, under cold conditions the fish often respond better once the sun has been on the water for awhile.

Is the sun in their eyes? If the sun is straight upstream so it shines directly in the steelhead's eyes, fishing in that run will be poor.

Temperature and turbidity. When the water temperature is low, say under 42 degrees, steelhead are often found in somewhat slower water than usual. When the river is muddy, steelhead tend to move to slower water near the bank.

Lead, don't follow. When using a classic wet fly swing, lead the fly slightly with the rod. Otherwise the fly will tend to drag.

Stack mend for quicker sink. When fishing a weighted fly (with or without an indicator) and a floating line, do a "stack mend" just after the fly hits the water: throw out some extra line so it piles on top of the indicator or the line/leader knot. This reduces drag and helps the fly sink more quickly.

Don't cast to your limit. A common mistake of beginning steelheaders is to try to cast as far as they can. Usually this results in about one good cast out of every five. Unfortunately, the four bad casts spooked the fish, so the one decent cast does no good. You'll hook more steelhead with consistently clean casts, even if they are shorter.

Following fish. Steelhead often follow a fly before they strike it. This means that the place you hook a steelhead usually is not the place the steelhead was lying.

Watch for boils and flashes. Steelhead often follow the fly, then don't take it. However, a fish that moves will probably take your fly if it's given another chance. So watch for boils or flashes by your fly. If you see one but don't get a grab, cast again. You'll probably get a hookup.

Dealing with plucks. Sometimes a following fish will strike a fly and not get hooked. All you feel is a quick, hard pluck at your line. Most of those fish can be hooked if you cast again to the same place. If you cast again and nothing happens, take a couple of steps upstream and come down on the fish again. If that doesn't work, tie on a smaller, darker fly and try again.

Swing, don't strike. When you're using a classic wet fly presentation, steelhead will follow the fly, grab it, turn, and return to their lie. This means they will naturally pull the fly into the corner of their jaw, securely hooking themselves. Let them do it! If you strike too quickly, you may pull the fly from the fish's mouth before it has a chance to turn and hook itself. So when you first begin to feel a pull, don't strike. Instead, swing your rod toward shore (away from the fish). This works best if you have a loop of about 18 inches of fly line between the reel and your forefinger; let the loop slip through your finger as you swing the rod.

Downstream takes. It is very common for steelhead to follow a fly until it stops swinging, then grab it. Unfortunately, the fly is now directly below the angler, who lifts the rod quickly as soon as the fish pulls. Of course the fly is immediately jerked out of the steelhead's mouth and, once again, defeat is snatched from the jaws of victory. When you get a downstream take, release the loop of line (see above) and push the rod toward the steelhead. This gives the fish enough slack to turn and hook itself. (Only about 5% of steelheaders have the presence of mind to actually do this; I belong to the other 95%.)

Guides. Fly rod steelheading is tough to do well, and a beginner can spend days, even seasons, mastering a few basic techniques. Fishing with a professional guide can shorten the learning curve and save a lot of futile effort. Even many expert anglers will hire a guide if they are visiting a new river. These anglers know that selecting the right water at the right time is 90% of the game, and a good guide will put them on the best water. After a day or two, this angler will have a good feel for the river and can fish confidently without a guide.

Winter Steelheading

When the water temperature drops below 50 degrees, steelhead tend to hug the bottom and won't move very far to take a fly. In most winter conditions, the water is often colder than that, usually between 38 and 46 degrees. Under those conditions, steelhead will seldom move more than 12-18 inches to intercept a fly. This means your fly has to be presented near the bottom and just about bonk Mr. and Ms. Steelhead on the nose. Two of the tactics discussed earlier work quite well when fly fishing for winter steelhead: a sink-tip line, and the deep dead drift that relies on a floating line.

A sink-tip line lets you fish much the same way you'd fish with traditional floating line tactics. To take full advantage of this method, carry sink-tip lines in several densities so you can adjust to different depths and current speeds. Fly lines with a built-in sink-tip, such as the Teeny Nymph lines, are convenient, but they limit you to only one density per reel spool. Another approach is to use a thin running line with interchangeable sink-tip heads of different densities. A good fly shop can put together a sink-tip system for you.

While sink-tip tactics work on single-handed fly rods, they are even better on two-handed rods. There are four reasons to use a two-handed spey rod: first, it's a lot easier on your shoulders because you use two arms to cast that heavy line; second, it's more efficient because you don't have to pull in a lot of line before casting; third, you have better line control and can mend better; and last, it's fun and the current cool thing to do.

The sink-tip method is not the only tactic for winter fish, however. The deep dead drift tactic is also very effective when fishing slots and pocket water, and it is especially suited to small streams, such as you often find on the coast.

When looking for a good place to chase winter steelhead with a fly, choose a river with these qualities:

Not too deep. Stick to rivers where you can find steelhead in less than eight feet of water. Less than six feet is better.

Not too wide. Even with a spey rod, most anglers can't hope to cast much beyond 75-80 feet with a sink-tip line. The dead drift tactic is even more limited. So you need a river that is on the smallish side, or at least one where the steelhead are easily reached from the bank or from a boat.

Not too crowded. If there are two dozen guys with drift gear standing shoulder to shoulder, and you move in with your fly rod . . . well, let's just say the consequences will not be pretty. A fly rodder needs room, so seek out the less populated rivers and runs.

Once you've selected a river, the next step is to find good runs. Basically, you look for the same things you looked for when fishing for summer steelhead, except when the water is cold you find steelhead in somewhat slower water.

One final piece of advice about winter steelheading: recognize that you are at the mercy of the weather. If the rivers are high and off-color, no one will do well, and a fly rodder is at an even bigger disadvantage than an angler with drift gear. Some days — —a *lot* of days—you're better off to stay home, tie some flies by the fire, and dream of clearing, dropping rivers.

A winter steelhead from a small stream.

Lower Deschutes River—Steelhead

If you love to swing a wet fly in the classic manner, this your river. The long runs, excellent holding water, and (at least in recent years) large numbers of fish make the Deschutes one of the premier steelhead fisheries in the lower 48. Throw in the beauty of the deep basalt-ribbed canyon and abundant sunshine, and you have the stuff of dreams.

Access and Facilities

See the "Trout" section for access and facilities, as well as maps of the river above Macks Canyon.

When to Fish

Steelhead begin entering the Deschutes in early July. Fresh fish continue to arrive through the end of the year. They gradually spread throughout the river, and by the end of September steelhead are in fishable numbers as far up as Warm Springs.

Species

Not very long ago, the Deschutes had a healthy run of wild native steelhead that spawned in Trout Creek and other tributaries. Currently, however, the wild fish are in trouble, and most of the steelhead are hatchery fish. In fact, most of them can't even call the Deschutes home—they are strays from other river systems. A recent sampling at Sherars Falls showed that 75% of the steelhead trapped there were stray fish from other hatcheries.

Deschutes River
Macks Canyon to the Mouth

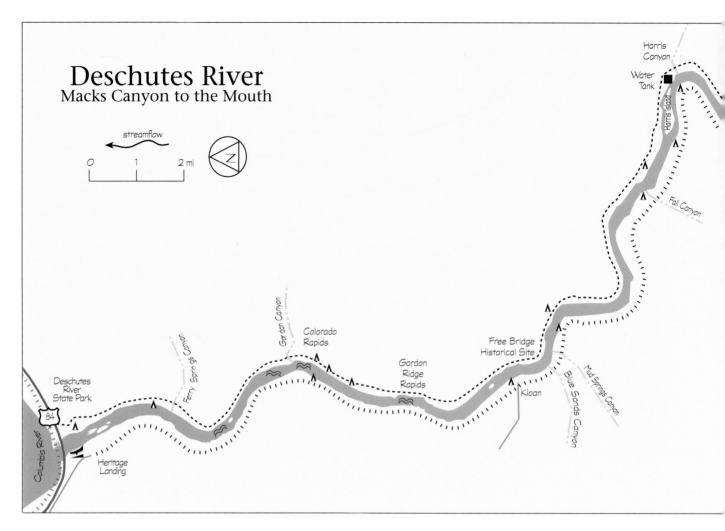

There are several reasons for this. One is that steelhead are notorious for wandering off to river systems other than their home waters. Another is that the Deschutes offers a shot of cool, oxygenated water for steelhead swimming up the Columbia. So a steelhead that is bound for Idaho will duck into the Deschutes to get out of the Columbia's warm waters. That's why there are many more steelhead in the lower miles of the river than farther upstream. And why there is more fishing pressure below Macks Canyon.

Services

See the "Trout" section for services.

Fishing Tips

Classic water for classic tactics. The Deschutes is perfectly suited for traditional floating line steelhead tactics.

However . . . Under the bright midday sun, Deschutes steelhead usually head for deeper water, or pull up under the white water at the heads of riffles, or stay in their usual lies and refuse to move very far for a fly. They are not uncatchable, however. It takes a sink-tip line to reach them; they are still more reluctant than they will be when the sun dips below the rimrock, but they will sometimes take a fly. But you need the sink-tip, not a floating line. Or you could take a nap and wait for dusk.

Cold water. As the water cools below 50 degrees in the fall, fish are less willing to move to a fly, so you must get down deeper and meet them where they rest. This usually means going to a sink-tip line.

Spey rods. As on many Northwest rivers, spey

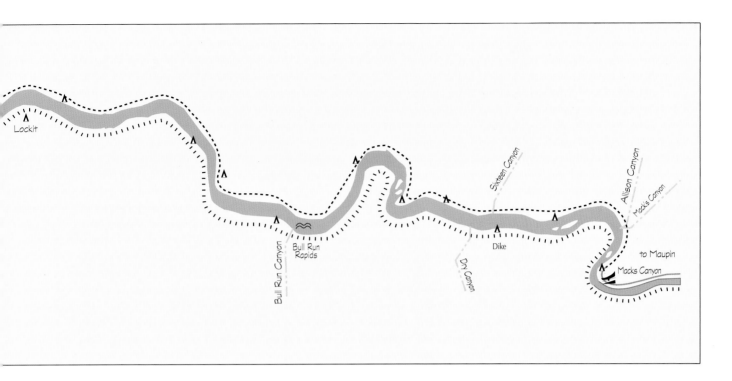

rods are increasingly popular on the Deschutes. The two-handed rods let you cast farther, especially when backcast room is limited.

Camp Water. When someone has pitched a tent beside a run, it is their camp water. It is considered bad form to fish someone else's camp water without asking them first. Violations of this etiquette can lead to strong words, or worse.

Pressure. A lot of people fish here, and angling pressure can be strong, especially on the lower twelve miles of the river. There can be a strong "me-first" feeling, with aggressive tendencies coming to the fore. Put them aside; patience and good manners will make your trip more enjoyable.

Special Regulations

Artificial flies and lures only. No angling from a floating device. No wild (not fin-clipped) steelhead may be kept. Boaters Pass required to float any portion. A special permit is required to fish the Warm Springs Reservation section. There are special rules (too complicated and variable to repeat here) for boaters below Macks Canyon.

Freight Train
(Randall Kaufmann)

Hook:	7999, sizes 2-6
Thread:	Black
Wing:	White calftail with pearl Krystal Flash
Rib:	Fine oval silver tinsel
Body:	In sequence, from back to front: fire orange fuzzy wool, red fuzzy wool, black chenille
Hackle:	Purple

This can also be tied with an all Krystal Flash wing.

North Umpqua River

The Deschutes and North Umpqua rivers form the yin and yang of Oregon steelheading. The Deschutes is in a desert, while the North Umpqua is forested. The Deschutes is big and brawling, the North Umpqua is tight and intimate. The Deschutes has long, classic runs, the North Umpqua has many small pools and pockets. But the two rivers have common qualities, too. They both have good runs of powerful steelhead, they are both world famous, and above all, they both evoke strong feelings among anglers.

Many of the North Umpqua's anglers regard the river as a sort of temple of steelheading, a shrine in which to worship, contemplate, and seek renewal. Many also regard themselves as self-appointed priests and arbiters of what is and is not proper steelheading dogma. It's just that kind of place; it has a powerful effect on people's emotions.

Emotions aren't the only strong, conflicting forces here. The river's current packs a powerful wallop. The North Umpqua is a "structure" river, with many ledges, sudden drops, troughs, and other bedrock phenomena. This is part of its beauty, and also why it is so suited to steelhead. It is also why it is hard to fish. The structure creates very tricky, often conflicting currents that make it difficult for a fly to get a good drift or to reach the level of a resting steelhead.

So like most religious experiences, there's nothing simple or obvious about fishing the North Umpqua. But once you've tied into one of its elusive steelhead, you'll never be the same again.

Access and Facilities

Hwy. 138 runs between I-5 on the west and Hwy. 97 to the east, paralleling the north bank of the North Umpqua much of the way. There are frequent turn-outs where anglers can park their cars and scramble down the steep bank to the river. The south bank can be reached by one of several bridges across the river. Most bridges have parking areas on the south bank, and trails that lead upstream and down. So bank access is straightforward here, but it takes more shoe leather to reach the south bank, hence that side is not fished as much.

Douglas County maintains several "waysides" along the river. These have parking, picnic facilities, and toilets. There are also several riverside campgrounds, including Susan Creek (which has showers), Bogus Creek, Island, Horseshoe Bend, Eagle Rock, and Boulder Flat.

Services

Roseburg, near the North Umpqua's junction with the mainstem of the Umpqua, has restaurants, motels, and other services. There are also a few inexpensive motels along Hwy 138. The Steamboat Inn, in the middle of the fly-water section, is a center of casual good taste; it is world-famous for it's fine food and lodging. During the day, the Inn is open to the public for breakfast and lunch, and you don't have to be an overnight guest to make a reservation for one of its famous dinners.

Joe Howell's Blue Heron fly shop is in Idleyld. Joe carries a large selection of non-imported steelhead flies. Some flies and tackle are also available at the Steamboat Inn.

Species

Although summer steelhead get most of the attention here, winter steelhead make a strong showing as well. So there is hardly a month when fresh fish are not nosing into the river. About half the steelhead in the fly fishing section are wild native fish; most of them spawn in Steamboat Creek. The typical steelhead has spent two years in the ocean

Green Butt Skunk
(Dan Callahan)

Hook:	7999, sizes 2-6
Thread:	Black
Wing:	White calftail
Butt:	Green chenille
Rib:	Fine oval silver tinsel
Body:	Black chenille
Hackle:	Black

Probably the most popular steelhead fly in the Northwest. Sizes 2 and 6 are the most useful.

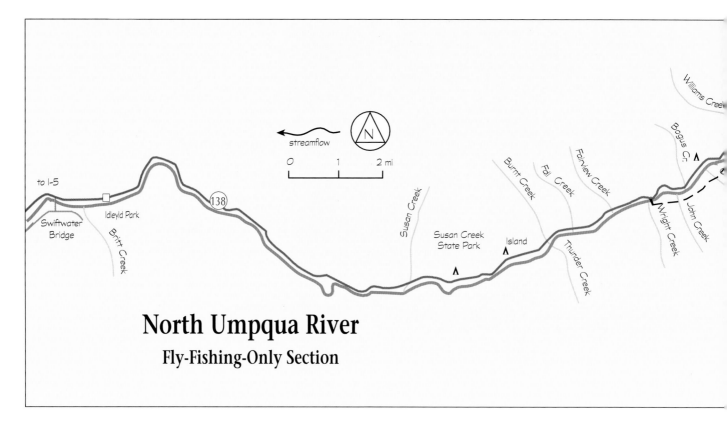

North Umpqua River
Fly-Fishing-Only Section

and weighs eight or nine pounds.

Besides steelhead, the river holds large numbers of spring and fall chinook. They are often seen resting in the backeddies or digging redds in September. The searun cutthroat population has declined so drastically that fishing for any species of trout is not permitted in the North Umpqua.

When to Fish

Fish the North Umpqua anytime it's not too high and you can get there. There are always fresh bright steelhead in the river. Of course, some months are better than others. July through mid-October are best for summer runs; March and April are best for winter fish. Mid-October through July, the biggest problems are river conditions, not lack of fish. During those months the river can be very cold or high and off-color. Sometimes there are mild, dry Novembers when the river is full of fish and empty of anglers.

Fishing Tips

Geology is destiny. The North Umpqua's ledgey, rocky structure governs the fishing.

While the river has some classic runs that call out for a traditional wet-fly swing, it also has lots of pocket water that cries for a different approach. All the tactics discussed in the "Steelhead Tips" chapter have a place here.

Light is not a factor late in the year. Throughout the summer, fishing is best at dawn and dusk. But by October the sun is low enough that the canyon blocks most of the direct light, and you can fish until you drop.

Cleats are essential. The river has ledges, sudden drop offs, and strong, tricky currents. Take them seriously. Wear stream cleats or boots with studs. No exceptions. A wading staff is also a good idea.

Bland flies for jaded fish. When the skies have been dry for awhile and steelhead have not moved, use a small fly (size 10 or 12) in a bland color such as tan or brown. Present it like you were nymphing for trout.

Mott Trail. The Mott Trail between Mott Bridge and Wright Creek makes a nice daylong trip, if you can handle a five-mile walk and can get someone to shuttle you back to your car. Once you're out of the "Camp

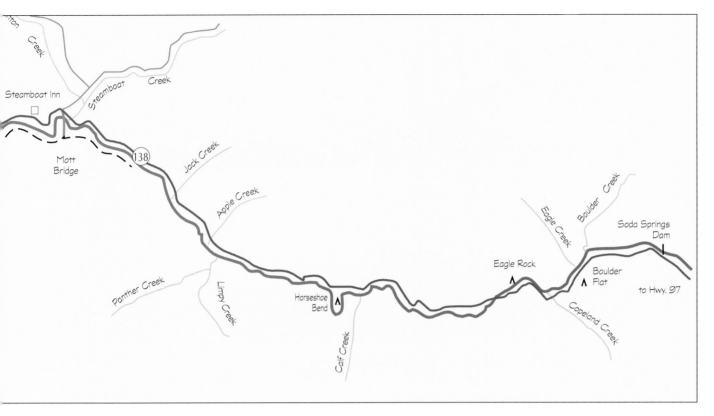

Water" near the Steamboat Inn, the best fishing is in the middle of the journey.

Don't just fish the famous runs. There are many famous steelhead runs on this river, but only about 20% of the good water has a name. So forget those maps with little numbers and names dotting the river. Find your own runs and give them a name known only to you. Turnouts are frequent along Hwy 138. They're almost always near good water, so they make a good starting point.

Opinions run strong. With such a variety of water, there are a variety of techniques that work well. Throw in the aesthetic virtues of the river, and you have a recipe for strong opinions of a religious nature, such as what is and is not "proper" fly fishing. If you want to start a heated argument, have dinner at the Steamboat Inn and mention to the anglers at your table that you hooked three fish while using an indicator rig.

Watch for log trucks. Hwy 138 is a major thoroughfare for log trucks, and they have little patience with anglers who dawdle along the road looking for good fly water.

Set your expectations. This is some of the most difficult steelhead water in the world. Hooking a fish is tough, and landing one is even harder.

Summer warmth. It can get over 100 degrees in the canyon in summer.

Watch your rod. As with many fisheries where a road parallels the river, anglers often use magnetic rod racks attached to the outside of their cars. If you use one, never leave a rod unattended. It's too tempting to someone driving by.

Special Regulations

Artificial flies with barbless hooks only from boundary near Swiftwater Bridge to near Soda Springs Dam (over 30 miles). No angling from a floating device. Closed to trout fishing. Only fin-clipped steelhead may be kept. All tributaries are closed to angling.

Grande Ronde River

Remote and isolated, the Grande Ronde is seldom experienced by most Oregon steelheaders. For the majority of the state this is a long, long drive—seven hours or more from Portland. And as far as the river's fans are concerned, that's just fine; they'd like to keep this gem to themselves.

The Grande Ronde is reminiscent of the Deschutes, although it is much smaller, per- haps a third the size. And the vegetation is different: firs and pines rather than sage and juniper. Like the Deschutes, however, this is a classic step-cast-swing river. Most of the runs are easily read by an experienced angler. The best fly rodding is in October and early November and is concentrated near the tiny town of Troy.

Access and Facilities

Most Oregon anglers will reach the lower Grande Ronde by taking Hwy. 3 from Enterprise. This road climbs to an elevation of 4,600 feet, then twists and turns as it drops almost 3,000 feet into the canyon of the Grande Ronde. At the bottom take the road to Troy, which follows the river and reaches town in seven miles.

The Troy road gives access to the river's west bank. There are frequent turn-outs for parking your car. Just above Troy, the road swings away from the river, then comes back to it and follows the bank another seven miles. Then the road crosses a bridge, and anglers no longer have bank access.

There is a bridge at Troy, and a road goes down the south bank before turning up the hill. This road gives good access to about a mile of the south bank.

Some visitors to the Grande Ronde look at the map and see a "short cut" road between Elgin and Troy. Don't take it. It's a steep, twisting gravel road whose natural hazards are made worse by a few crazed hunters who roar up and down it like they were the only people on earth. Those who know the area don't use this road in fall.

There are several places to camp along the river, including a grassy field just downstream from Troy. Expect no facilities whatsoever. The store in Troy has pay showers. There is an RV park at Troy.

While the Grande Ronde is mostly a bank fishing experience, a few people take drift boats here. There are launch points at Troy and at the bridge above town. But really, a boat is more trouble than it's worth in the Troy area. The river is small and intimate, so a boat just causes conflicts and problems. There are some who feel fishing from a boat should be outlawed on this stretch. A pontoon craft, however, can be handy for reaching a few spots that fish best from the east bank.

A few very hardy (and maybe foolhardy) anglers make a fall drift from Minam to Troy, a distance of 47 miles through an isolated wilderness. Since it is mid- to late-November before large numbers of steelhead reach that far upstream, the weather is likely to be un-pleasant, even dangerous. And the nights are long, cold, and dark. And the fish might not be there anyway. But if you really want to do it, you need river flows of at least 1,100 cfs if you're rafting, and 2,500 cfs if you're in a drift boat. You need to carry a portable toilet, a fire pan, and pack out your ashes.

Services

Troy is an exceedingly small town. It has a store with the bare necessities, maybe. There is also a restaurant and a "hunting lodge" that harkens to days of yore. John Ecklund's Grande Ronde Lodge, however, is a classy facility about four miles downstream from town. It caters to fly anglers and offers guides, lodging, and fine meals in a large log lodge (call 541/963-7878 for bookings). The lodge also has flies and limited tackle.

Streetwalker
(Gordon Nash)

Hook:	7999, sizes 2-6
Thread:	Black
Tail:	Purple hackle fibers
Wing:	Pearl Flashabou
Rib:	Fine silver tinsel
Body:	Purple chenille
Hackle:	Purple

I love the way this fly looks in the water, especially under low light. And so do steelhead. It is a variation of the the Purple Peril, which has a wing made from fox squirrel.

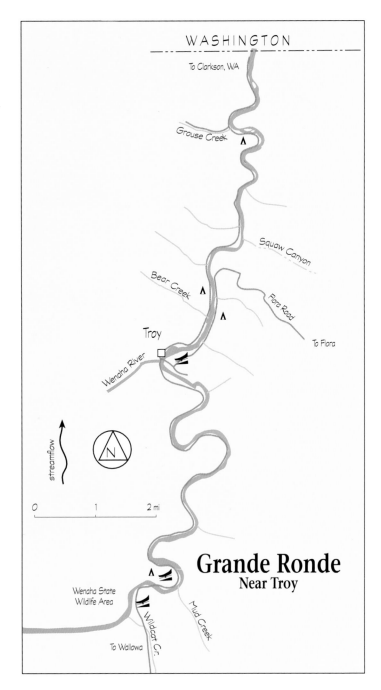

weather has worsened, and fishing tapers off. But in the six-week window, fishing can be excellent. After mid-November, weather is a major factor, and it is possible to get marooned by a snow storm.

Fishing Tips

Runs are easy to spot. The Grande Ronde is a classic steelhead river that is well suited to traditional tactics. A newcomer with some experience should not have a hard time figuring out where the runs are.

Fish respond well in low temperatures. In early October, the river temperature is usually between 45 and 50 degrees. Even so, the steelhead respond well to a fly presented on a floating line.

When to use a sink-tip. As the water temperature drops below 45 degrees, a sink-tip line works better.

Respect private property. Although most of the river bank is in private hands, anglers are seldom confronted with "No Trespassing" signs. That will change, however, if they act inconsiderately, litter, or damage fences and gates.

Banker's hours. The river seldom turns on before 10 a.m., and the best fishing is between then and 3 p.m.

Get a Washington license. Seven miles below Troy, the Grande Ronde crosses the border into Washington and flows on to the Snake River. There is plenty of good fishing along the Washington section, and a visiting angler would be wise to get a Washington license and fish it.

Special Regulations

Only fin-clipped *trout* may be kept.

Species

The Grande Ronde's steelhead are summer-run fish, mostly of hatchery origin. About 10% of the run is wild steelhead.

When to Fish

These fish have to travel 800 miles up the Columbia and Snake rivers to get here, so fishing doesn't get underway until October. By mid-November, the river has cooled,

Rogue River

The Rogue is a river of legend. First popularized by the writings of Zane Grey, it became home to movie stars who liked to fish. Ginger Rogers had a ranch here, as did Clark Gable. But the biggest celebrities are the river's fish. Abundant runs of wild steelhead and salmon still swim here, and anglers often go home happy and satisfied.

Like an actor, the Rogue is capable of playing several character roles. From its source near Crater Lake to its mouth at the Pacific Ocean, it is at turns a pretty mountain creek, a broad river, a slow-moving urban waterway, and a deep, fast flowing canyon-bound cataract.

The Upper Rogue, between Lost Creek Dam and Gold Ray Dam, has the best fly fishing. This section is centered on the town of Shady Cove

Access and Facilities

Hwy. 62 parallels the Upper Rogue above the town of Shady Cove, and there are occasional turnouts and public parks that give bank access to the river. Below Shady Cove, access is less frequent, and bank anglers will find only a couple of spots from which to fish.

In general, bank fishing is marginal on the Upper Rogue, and boaters will find more

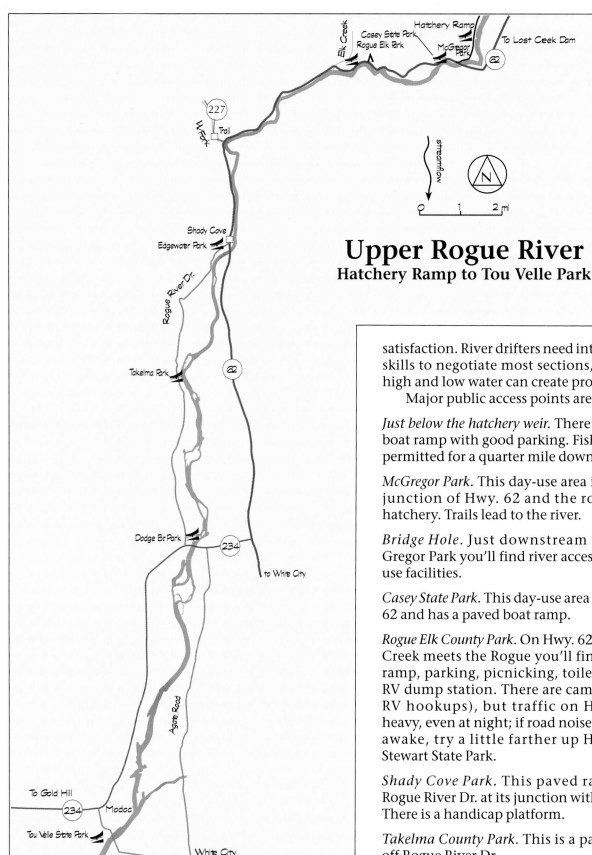

Upper Rogue River
Hatchery Ramp to Tou Velle Park

satisfaction. River drifters need intermediate skills to negotiate most sections, and both high and low water can create problems.

Major public access points are:

Just below the hatchery weir. There is a gravel boat ramp with good parking. Fishing is not permitted for a quarter mile downstream.

McGregor Park. This day-use area is near the junction of Hwy. 62 and the road to the hatchery. Trails lead to the river.

Bridge Hole. Just downstream from Mc-Gregor Park you'll find river access and day-use facilities.

Casey State Park. This day-use area is on Hwy. 62 and has a paved boat ramp.

Rogue Elk County Park. On Hwy. 62 where Elk Creek meets the Rogue you'll find a paved ramp, parking, picnicking, toilets, and an RV dump station. There are campsites (no RV hookups), but traffic on Hwy. 62 is heavy, even at night; if road noise keeps you awake, try a little farther up Hwy. 62 at Stewart State Park.

Shady Cove Park. This paved ramp is on Rogue River Dr. at its junction with Hwy. 62. There is a handicap platform.

Takelma County Park. This is a paved ramp off Rogue River Dr.

Dodge Bridge. Another paved ramp off Rogue River Dr. at its junction with Hwy. 234. There is a handicap platform.

Modoc. This is a brushy, litter-strewn, primitive area off Modoc Rd. It has several points of bank access and a crude dirt boat ramp. Break-ins are frequent, so never let your car out of your sight. Under no circumstances whatsoever should you even think about camping here.

Tou Velle State Park. The park is off Table Rock Rd. The river splits it in two, with a pleasant picnic area on the south side, and a paved boat ramp on the north bank. Tou Velle Park is the last take-out point for river drifters. The Rogue is free-flowing for another three miles to Gold Ray Dam, but only jet boats can make the trip because there is no take-out at Gold Ray.

Services

Both Medford and Grants Pass are within an hour's drive and have extensive visitor services. Ashland is not far away, either. Shady Cove has restaurants and stores, and there are several RV parks along the river. People who use motels seem to prefer staying in Medford rather than Shady Cove.

The Fishin' Hole in Shady Cove has flies and some supplies, as well as a guide service. There are full-service fly shops in Medford and Ashland.

Species

The Rogue's steelhead have a life-history that is unique to the Rogue and two other rivers, the Klamath and the Eel. Like most steelhead, smolts head to the ocean, but unlike all other strains, they come back in the fall as immature fish of about 12-16 inches. These are the famous Rogue half-pounders. They hang around the river, feeding like trout, then head back to the ocean. When they come back again, they are sexually mature steelhead, ready to spawn.

Because they spend less time feeding in the ocean, the Rogue's summer steelhead are smaller than steelhead in other rivers. A typical mature fish is 18-22 inches and weighs 2-3 pounds. However, there are also many fish that go five, six, or even ten pounds.

About half the summer steelhead are wild fish, and even hatchery fish are descended from the river's wild strain. Summer steelhead begin entering the river in May, and by July there is good angling on the Upper Rogue. The bulk of the run arrives in September and October. Hatchery fish are often captured at the hatchery weir, then trucked back to Gold Ray Dam and released for anglers to have another go at them.

Bright winter steelhead can be found in the Upper Rogue from December through April. Over 80% of the winter fish are wild native steelhead. They tend to be larger than the summer-run fish.

The Rogue also supports substantial wild native populations of spring and fall chinook salmon. Spawning salmon are often found in the Upper Rogue from August through October, and this can affect the fishing (see the section on Fishing Tips).

When to Fish

There is hardly a month when fresh steelhead cannot be found in the Upper Rogue. However, the best months are September and October for summer fish, and February through mid-April for winter fish. In September and October, the river is an "artificial fly" water. In ODFW-speak, that means people can fish with a spinning rod and a bubble, if a fly is tied on. However, most people use normal fly gear.

Fishing Tips

The structure is different. This is not the Deschutes. There is no canyon, and few long runs. The river is often shallow, but has many boulders, trenches, slots, drop-offs, and ledges. This means you are almost always fishing pocket water, not long, classic step-cast-swing runs.

The temperature is different. During the peak September-October fishing season, you will be fishing winter-like water temperatures of about 45 degrees. Under these conditions, most fish will be found near the bottom and will not move very far for a fly. To be effective, you need gear and tactics that will reach the bottom.

The fish are different. Because so many of the Rogue's steelhead have a half-pounder life-history, they feed like trout when they enter the river. It is not unusual to see big steel-head doing head-and-tail rises as they take caddis pupae during a fall hatch. Because they feed so readily, the Rogue's steelhead are receptive to trout patterns such as a stonefly nymph or a caddis pupa drifted near the bottom.

Spawning salmon are different. From late September through October, the Upper Rogue is full of spawning salmon. When the salmon are on their redds, you will usually find steelhead a few yards below them waiting to ingest salmon roe. For this reason, egg flies are very effective at that time of year.

Putting it together. Add up the differences—structure, temperature, fish behavior, spawning salmon—and you need tactics other than a traditional wet-fly swing. The most effective tactic on the Rogue is the Deep Dead Drift method discussed in the Steelhead Tips chapter. In September, use a pattern such as the Big Bird (it looks like a caddis pupa), and in October use an egg fly either singly or as a trailer in a two-fly rig. There are places and times when traditional techniques work here, but the best tactic is usually a smallish fly dead-drifted near the bottom. In October look for spawning salmon, and cast an egg fly right on top them. It will reach the bottom behind them, and drift into the mouth of a waiting steel-head.

Big Bird
(Mike St. John)

Hook: 5262, sizes 8-12
Thread: Brown
Tail: Grizzly hen hackle fibers
Wire: Fine copper
Body: Tan Haretron
Hackle: Grizzly hen saddle

Steelhead sometimes prefer a drab fly presented on a dead drift. This is a great pattern for those times. It should be fished near the bottom on an indicator rig. It's a killer on the Rogue, but it produces well in other places, too. Always tie it with the bead head.

Special Regulations

Barbless artificial flies only September and October; no added weights. Only fin-clipped steelhead may be kept. Check regulations for additional restrictions.

Other Useful Information

Additional Pursuits: Bass and Shad

While trout and steelhead get the lion's share of attention from Oregon fly anglers, other species of fish are worth pursuing as well. Some adventurous fly rodders are going after powerful spring chinook, while others are pioneering saltwater opportunities such as surf perch, ling cod from a jetty, and sea bass from offshore charter boats. Sadly, some of our best fly fishing opportunities of past years—coho salmon and searun cutthroat—are rarely available to us now. Habitat loss and poor ocean feeding conditions have devastated these once-abundant fisheries. While there are a few places that occasionally have strong runs of coho and searuns, their status is fragile, and I can't recommend them. Another fly fishery that has fallen on hard times is chum salmon.

However, some non-native species are thriving. Smallmouth bass, largemouth bass, and shad are good sport on a fly rod, and are the focus of this chapter.

Smallmouth Bass

It was Dave's turn to row the drift boat while I cast a small popper into mini-backeddies along a basalt cliff on the John Day River. I would cast so my popper landed a few inches from the cliff, let it settle a bit, then give it a twitch. On nearly every cast, a smallmouth bass would slam the popper.

Different season, different river—September on the mainstem of the Umpqua. I dropped the anchor in a rocky pool. In the clear water, Martin and I could see curious smallmouth bass come near the boat. Martin lowered a stonefly nymph, jigged it a couple of times, then let it drop onto the bottom. He watched carefully as a 20-inch bass neared it, then sucked it off the bottom. Later, as he released the fish, he said, "You never feel a thing. If you couldn't see those fish, you'd never hook them."

Bass are not native to Oregon. Somehow, smallmouth bass became established, and on rivers such as the Umpqua, John Day, and

An Umpqua smallmouth from near the Big K Ranch.

a few others, they are abundant and provide good sport for fly anglers. The best places to find them are near structure, such as logs, the edges of weedbeds, drop-offs, points of land, rocks, docks, places that form backeddies, etc. Other than the spawning season, they prefer to be in or near current. They are not wanderers, so once you find a concentration of smallmouth, you can just keep coming back to the same place. While they don't mind cover (snags, weeds, etc.), it is not essential to them. Bass are inactive during the winter, but once the water warms above 60 degrees, fishing can be excellent.

The best flies and tactics for smallmouth vary. Surface poppers work great on the John Day, but not on the Umpqua. On the other hand, the sight-fishing that works so well on the Umpqua won't do much for you on the

John Day. A tactic that works well on most rivers is to present a streamer or baitfish pattern, such as a silver Zonker, on a sinking line; vary the depth until you find a combination that works. Woolly Buggers are also productive; black and brown are good colors, and chartreuse can be very effective.

Here are some good places to fish for smallmouth bass.

John Day River. While you can occasionally find a fish over three pounds, most are 8-12 inches. But there are lots of them. You need a driftboat or raft for most of the river, but there is some bank access near Spray and at the boat ramps. Popular drifts are Service Creek to Twickenham (one day) and Twickenham to Clarno (another two days).

Umpqua River. The mainstem (below Roseburg) has excellent fishing, with some fish over four pounds. Some of the quieter pools are suitable for pontoon boats. The stretch through the Big K Ranch (near Elkton) has excellent fishing, but you need to be a guest (it's worth the money; you get about 12 miles of essentially private water).

Willamette River. From Newberg downstream through the Multnomah Channel, you can find good smallmouth fishing. Seek areas where some kind of structure breaks a moderate current. The mouths of tributary rivers can be good places. Except for the spawning season, you'll find very few bass in the back bays.

Columbia River. Stick to the edges of the main river, not the ponds and sloughs.

Hagg Lake. This close-to-Portland stillwater has produced several state record smallmouth (but not on fly gear).

Brownlee Reservoir. Fishing can be outstanding on grasshopper patterns if there is an outbreak of grasshoppers in the area.

Largemouth Bass

"You live for the grab," a fly angler once confided to me. I think that's especially true of largemouth bass. Pound-for-pound, I'm not impressed with them as a fighting fish, but that first grab and run can be a real rush, especially if ol' bucketmouth took a big popper off the surface. And largemouth can get big and will jump, so that makes up for their lack of endurance.

As with smallmouth, largemouth bass fishing is best when the water has warmed past 60 degrees. In spring, you find male largemouth in the shallow margins of lakes, building and guarding nests. The big females cruise in, lay their eggs, then leave. The males stay and guard the nest. That's why you should never keep bass during the spawning season: with no male to guard the nest, the progeny will be probably be lost.

Once the spawning season is over, largemouth will spread around the lake. They are wanderers, cruising wide areas in search of food and good conditions. They favor the same kind of structure as smallmouth (see above), but they want cover as well. Cover includes weed beds, overhead logs, docks, etc. In summer, morning and evening are the best times, and fishing after dark can sometimes be productive. Fishing can slow in August, but as the water cools in fall it can turn on again—until the water temperature drops below 60.

Surface poppers, Woolly Buggers, and Zonkers are all good flies. I'm fond of poppers and use larger ones than I do for smallmouth. While I might tie an occasional deer hair popper, I usually use wood ones that I buy. When buying poppers, look for ones that are sparse (not over dressed), and have the eye at the bottom of the face. The back of the popper should settle into the water so the hook points upwards. The hook should be long-shanked and not immediately under the body. It takes a 7- or 8-weight rod to cast these big, air-resistant bugs. A bass-taper fly line and a short heavy leader help, too.

When fishing with a popper, sound is important. Experiment with different jerks and twitches, and remember the splash patterns and sound made by each. Sometimes a big splash attracts fish, but other days it scares them. Some days it's best to let your popper sit, with just an occasional twitch; other days you'll pick up more fish with a steady, noisy retrieve. Experiment, and when you find a combination that works, keep doing it.

Here are a few good places to find largemouth bass.

Mid-coast lakes. Ten Mile Lakes, Siltcoos Lake, and other lakes near Coos Bay and Florence have excellent largemouth fisheries. From April through fall you can find good fishing in areas with structure and cover.

Columbia/Willamette. Multnomah channel and Scappoose Bay are two good spots.

Reservoirs. Doreena, Cottage Grove, and Fern Ridge all have good largemouth fisheries.

Shad

Shad are an east coast import introduced to the San Francisco area about a century ago. They migrated north to Oregon and are established in several rivers, with some runs totalling over a million fish.

Shad are anadromous, like salmon and steelhead, and return from the ocean to spawn in freshwater. Females are the biggest, weighing three or four pounds. Male or female, they are one of the hardest fighting fish you'll find.

Shad migrate upriver in late spring. Mid-May through mid-June is usually best, but fish can be caught through early July. They are a schooling fish and are reluctant to take a fly or lure except in places where they stack up. Favorite gathering places are just below obstructions such as dams and large rapids, at creek mouths, and in depressions or pools. The vast majority of fish prefer water with a moderate to strong current.

These "way stations" can hold unbelievable numbers of fish, and it's useless to fish anywhere else. On an unfamiliar river, just keep cruising until you find a concentration of cars or boats. In fact, shad fishing can be an elbow-to-elbow experience, and some spots tend to be occupied by aggressive meat fisherman.

Shad flies are tied on small hooks (size 8-12) with enough weight to reach the fish.

Eastern Oregon largemouth bass. "Live for the grab."

Best colors are chartreuse, pink, white, and combinations of these. Keep the fly sparse. It helps to have a little something that wiggles, such as a bit of marabou. Some anglers (such as me) favor small curly-tail bass jigs. They're cheap, convenient, and work just dandy.

A six-weight rod is adequate. Some anglers prefer a sink-tip line, while others favor a floater and lots of weight on the fly and/or split shot on the leader. If the leader is too thick, the fly won't sink fast enough, so use 8-pound or less.

Position yourself a little to the side and slightly above the concentration of fish. Even a few feet can make the difference between an occasional hook-up and a fish on every cast.

Once you're in position, the trick is to get your fly down to the fish. Most of the time, it needs to drift near the bottom in places where shad stack up. Since the current can be strong in shad holes, flies should be weighted, and sometimes you need a couple of split shot on the leader.

Sink-tip lines are often used, but I usually prefer a floating line with a long leader and lots of weight on the fly; this gives me better line control. I like to start fishing about half-way to the bottom, then add weight until I find fish. As you might guess, casting a shad rig can be a danger to humanity, so you should either fish from a boat or find uncrowded water

Shad can hit the fly on the swing, while

Umpqua River shad. Note the deeply forked tail, a source of the fish's power.

it is drifting, or while it is sinking. I usually cast down-and-across and let the fly swing. If I don't get a hit, I'll feed out some line so the fly will sink down through the school. If there is still no hit, I retrieve in jerks (not too fast), occasionally stopping to let the fly sink. Once you find the right combination of position and presentation, just keep doing the same thing over and over.

Shad take the fly lightly, so it's important to have good line control and to manage your slack line. That way you'll feel the bite and be able to tighten up quickly. When you bring a fish to the boat, it's not unusual to see half a dozen other shad following the hooked fish.

Shad fishing is best under low light, so mornings and evenings are the best times.

Here are some Oregon rivers with big shad runs:

Umpqua main stem. Yellow Creek boat ramp, Sawyer Rapids, and the Big K Ranch are some of the good spots. You can gain easy access to Sawyer Rapids by paying a modest fee. The Big K Ranch is a private resort, so if crowds bother you and you don't mind spending the money for a few nights at the Big K, spring for it; it's a great facility and you essentially have private water at your disposal.

Willamette River. Below the Oregon City Falls (boat fishery only).

Columbia River. Below Bonneville or John Day dams.

Rogue River. Below Rainie Falls.

The tidewater section of the Coos River. This is a unique fishery because it is in tidewater, not the river itself.

Hatches and Other Trout Food

Quite a few years ago, I made my first fishing trip to Idaho. I'd been fly fishing seriously for half a dozen years, but this was the first time I'd ventured to the intermountain west. Each day at mid-morning, hoards of pale morning dun mayflies hatched in the spring creek, and eager trout rose to them. In the evening, the hatch repeated. Between hatches the trout would not feed, so it was pointless to cast a fly.

After two days of this, my main thought was: *So this is what all those magazines were talking about!* You see, I'd read a little about hatches and entomology, but I could rarely connect what I'd read to what I'd experienced in Oregon.

I know now that many of those articles were written by people who lived in the east, midwest, and intermountain west. And Oregon is different. Sometimes we have major hatches of mayflies, but other insects—midges, stoneflies, and caddis—are equally important. And when there's a mayfly hatch, it's seldom as massive as those described by writers who live farther east. Further, trout do a whole lot of feeding when there's no hatch at all. In fact, trout eat quite a few aquatic critters that are months, maybe years, from hatching. They even eat a lot of critters that aren't insects.

Therefore, when you fly fish in Oregon keep a few things in mind:

The four orders of aquatic insects most important to river anglers are mayflies, caddisflies, stoneflies, and midges. Each order is equally important. Anglers who suffer from mayfly myopia will net few fish.

A great deal of trout feeding has nothing to do with a hatch-in-progress. Anglers who want only to cast a dry fly during a hatch will spend a lot of time not fishing.

Oregon has a broad range of ecological and climatic zones. That means there is no month of the year when you can't catch trout on a fly—even on a dry fly.

This diversity also means that the species, timing, duration, nature, and intensity of hatches varies throughout the state.

Another fallout of ecological diversity is the diversity of aquatic life. Trout see a lot of different kinds of bugs, and they can get selective on any stage of any species. And that means finding out what the trout want can sometimes be difficult.

For more information

Anyone who writes about fishing does so from the perspective of their own experience. If they've never been here, they might think Oregon is the same as Michigan or Montana. Fortunately, there are good books written by people who live and fish here. These authors don't suffer from the "trout food=mayfly hatch" syndrome. Here are a few books I recommend.

Western Hatches by Dave Hughes and Rick Hafele. An in-depth guide to western aquatic insects, including fly patterns.

Western Streamside Guide by Dave Hughes. Sometimes referred to as "Western Hatches Lite," this small book is a good introduction to aquatic insects.

Hatch Guide for Western Streams by Jim Schollmeyer. This pocket-sized guide has lots of color photos that help anglers identify each stage of the most important insects and pick a fly that matches it.

Hatch Guide for Lakes by Jim Schollmeyer. Similar to the above book, but for stillwaters.

Aquatic Insects and Their Imitations, by Rick Hafele and Scott Roederer. This book has solid entomology and good illustrations, including keys for identifying aquatic insects.

The Pocket Gillie by Scott Richmond. A pocket-sized guide to essential fly fishing knowledge; features identification charts for nymphs (to the genus level for mayflies) and closely ties fishing tactics to entomology.

Common Oregon Trout Foods

I've summarized Oregon's most common trout foods below. I haven't included every possibility, just the ones anglers are most likely to encounter. The major hatches and other food are described first, then there is a chart listing aquatic insects and common imitations of them.

Northwest fly anglers are an odd lot, and when referring to hatches they often mix English common names with scientific Latin. Thus, one mayfly gets an English "green drake," but another species is given a Latin *"Baetis."* Still others get a nickname based on the Latin, such as "paralep" or "hex." I have a theory about this: anglers use whichever name has the fewest syllables.

To avoid confusion, I have listed insects by both the most common of their common names as well as their scientific genus.

Mayflies

Mayflies live underwater as nymphs until they reach maturity, then they hatch into winged adults called duns. The duns molt once more into a spinner that mates, then dies. Before dying, the females lay eggs in the river. A mayfly's adult life is brief, usually only a day or two.

Mayflies are sometimes divided into four major groups based on the behavior of the nymphs: crawlers, who spend their underwater life crawling between rocks and pebbles; clingers, who are flat little things that live in fast water and rarely lose their grip on the bottom; swimmers, who flip their tails and swim; and burrowers, who dwell in sediment.

Adult mayfly

The Oregon mayflies you are most likely to encounter are described below.

March Brown (*Rhithrogena*). March browns hatch in March and signal the beginning of spring (or, if you recently moved here from California, the middle of winter). They are a clinger type of mayfly, so the nymphs are rarely available to trout. The best hatches occur on rainy, miserable days shortly after noon. Willamette Valley rivers such as the McKenzie, as well as the middle Deschutes and a few other streams support significant March brown populations.

Mature nymphs often migrate to slower water before hatching. As the hatch begins, nymphs drift in the current, and trout will focus on this stage. Nymphs usually rise to the surface, where the dun hatches out and drifts briefly on the current before flying off (or being eaten by a trout); so when you see rises, a dry fly is probably the best choice. But sometimes emergence happens underwater and the dun floats to the surface. In this case a Soft Hackle or downwing wet fly works best.

Green Drake (*Drunella grandis* and *D. doddsi*). This large mayfly is adored by many fly anglers, although it is not widespread in Oregon. A crawler type of mayfly, green drake nymphs are often eaten by trout during the hatch season, and a nymph pattern such as the Poxyback Green Drake drifted near the bottom can produce fish several hours before the actual hatch. Because green drakes rarely hatch in large numbers, it is difficult to know where feeding trout are lying until you see a trout rise. Further, hatches occur on quiet runs, so a lot of blind casting will only spook the fish. Therefore the best strategy is to refrain from casting until you see a natural insect taken by a trout, then cast to that fish. The Metolius River has a noted hatch of green drakes.

Pale Morning Dun (*Ephemerella inermis* and *E. infrequens*). This small, pale yellow mayfly of the crawler group is usually referred to by its initials, PMD. Despite the name, most Oregon hatches occur in early afternoon. From mid-June through mid-July, this is the dominant hatch on most rivers. Trout take nymphs all day, and duns and emerging duns during the hatch. Best places are slow runs, backeddies, and under overhanging alders. Of the two species, *E. inermis* is much more numerous and is matched with a size 18 dry fly.

Yellow Quill (*Epeorus*). Also known as the

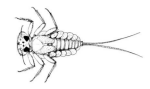
Yellow quill nymph

western Gordon quill, the yellow quill has baffled many Oregon fly anglers. The hatch occurs at the same season as the PMDs, and the dun is similar in appearance except it is bigger and the wing is yellow, not blue-gray. The trick here is that the dun hatches underwater and drifts to the surface, and trout prefer to take them underwater. Therefore a Soft Hackle is the right choice, not a dry fly. The yellow quill belongs to the clinger group, so the nymph is seldom available to trout. Hatches can be sporadic and often lack enough intensity to interest trout. But when it happens, you have to be prepared or you will be shut out.

Pale Evening Dun (Heptagenia). This guy looks a little like his morning counterpart, but is a bit bigger and has a body that is more tan than yellow; also, the wings are not smokey gray. PEDs are clinger mayflies, so the nymphs are seldom available to trout. When nearing maturity, they migrate towards quiet water near shore. Thus, hatches occur along the margins in slow water. Since trout in slow water near the bank are particularly wary, your casts need to be precise and targeted to individual fish.

Trico (Tricorythodes). Tricos are tiny mayflies with dark-hued bodies and white wings. Nymphs are not important, but hatches and spinner falls can trigger selective feeding. This insect's nickname, *the white-winged curse*, should serve as a warning. Trout can be maddeningly fussy about them, and everything that contributes to angling success is contradicted by harsh realities: imitations should ride as high in the water as possible, but without much hackle; tippets need to be 7X and long, but casts should be accurate and the leader needs to lie out straight; downstream presentations work best, but the wind is usually blowing upstream.

Trico males hatch at night when you can't fish for trout in Oregon. Females hatch in mid- to late-morning, and trout will take the duns during the hatch. Male and female spinners often fall onto the water at the same time, so spinner falls can be more massive than the hatch and therefore more important.

Slate-winged Olive (Drunella coloradensis). This species is similar to its larger cousin, the green drake. Hatches occur in July and August. Imitations are similar to those for the green drake, only smaller. Tactics are also similar.

Mahogany Dun (Paraleptophlebia). Along with the October caddis and the onset of the blue-winged olives, the mahogany duns (sometimes called "paraleps" by fly anglers) signal the coming of fall. Hatches are in September and October when many anglers are focused on steel-

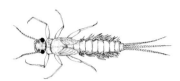
Mahogany dun nymph

head. Although the nymphs spend much of their lives in fast water, they migrate to slow water before emerging. Thus most hatches occur in slow, almost slack water near shore. Because the hatches are usually sputtering, sporadic events and because the duns drift a long while in slow water, trout will rise eagerly but not aggressively. For that reason this is a difficult hatch to fish well. As with the green drakes, don't cast until you know where a feeding fish is lying. A downstream presentation is usually best because the trout sees the fly before the line or leader. Trout will take nymphs, but the duns are much more important.

Blue-Winged Olive (Baetis, Diphetor, Pseudocloeon). These tiny mayflies rule the rivers half the year, the half most people don't fish. Most hatches begin in late September and continue until April, with the best activity in February and early March. I've never been to an Oregon river that didn't have a few blue-winged olives

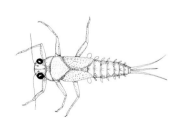
Blue-winged olive nymph

every winter afternoon. Hatches usually start about 1:30 or 2:00, with the best ones occurring on drizzly days. While slow runs can be good places to fish, most activity will be in backeddies, where little duns seem to circle endlessly—or until a trout sucks them down.

Nymph imitations are very productive when dead-drifted just above the bottom in slowish water. Emerger patterns are especially useful during the hatch, and spinner patterns can also be productive. When fishing a massive hatch, I use a dry fly that is slightly darker than the natural. The trout don't seem to care, and it's much easier to pick out my fly from the hundreds of naturals.

These insects are also called by their Latin name *Baetis* (usually pronounced *bait-us* by most fly anglers, although entomologists tell me *beet-us* is more correct and doesn't dredge up images of angle worms and salmon eggs).

Speckle-winged Quill (Callibaetis). This swimming mayfly is the dominant mayfly in lakes. Hatches begin as early as April or May and continue until the end of September. When the water is warm enough, eggs grow to mature nymphs in about six weeks. This means the insects get progressively smaller as the season wears on. In spring, duns are usually matched with a size 14 dry fly, but by fall, a size 16 or even 18 is needed.

Hatches usually start in mid-morning or early afternoon. While trout take the duns during the hatch (an Adams dry fly is a good choice), they also take the nymphs beginning a few hours before the onset, and continue taking them during and after the hatch. A Pheasant Tail Nymph is a good imitation of a *Callibaetis* nymph, but in my experience the Flashback Pheasant Tail outfishes a plain Pheasant Tail by three to one. When fishing nymphs, use an intermediate line, a long leader, and a very slow, steady retrieve. When using a dry fly, trim the hackle off the bottom so it is flush with the dubbing.

Hex; Big Yellow May (Hexagenia limbata). The largest of Oregon's mayflies, the *Hexagenia* is a burrower type that inhabits some lakes and slow sections of some rivers. Hatches usually occur in early July right at sunset. Lost Lake (Mt. Hood) and the Williamson River have noted *Hexagenia* hatches. Some of the mid-coast lakes such as Siltcoos and Eel have hex hatches, but they occur in May.

Nymphs can be productive when fished a couple of hours before the hatch. Go to water that is less than ten-feet deep. Use a weighted fly or lead on the leader, and let the fly settle to the bottom. Pull it up two or three feet, pause, then let it settle back down; repeat this several times before casting again. Hatches begin just before sunset, so take a flashlight with you. When you see duns on the surface, forget the nymph and fish a dry.

River-Dwelling Caddisflies

The caddisfly life-cycle is radically different from that of mayflies. First, caddis have an additional stage of development, changing from a larva to a pupa; the winged adult emerges from the pupa.

A second difference between caddis and mayflies is that the adult caddis emerges so quickly from the pupa that it is seldom available to trout during a hatch. However, the adult will live several weeks, spending much time in the alder trees and grass near the river bank. They often fall or are blown onto the water, where trout eat them. Therefore, while mayfly adults are mostly eaten by trout when they hatch, caddis adults are mostly eaten when they are *not* hatching.

A third difference is the manner in which eggs are laid. Some caddis species drop their eggs into the water from above, where trout can't get them. But many others crawl or swim to the bottom, deposit their eggs, then return to the surface. Throughout the egg-laying process they are vulnerable to trout.

Adult caddis

Finally, caddis are long-lived (compared to mayflies), vary in color even within the same species, and have overlapping hatch seasons. Therefore, on any day during the caddis season, trout are used to seeing adult caddis in a range of sizes and colors. This is good news for fly anglers. It means precise imitation is seldom necessary. "Close" is usually good enough when playing horseshoes or when tying caddis patterns.

By varying the hook size, body color, and wing color, caddis can be imitated with just a few fly patterns. A Sparkle Pupa or Soft Hackle imitates the pupal form. For adults, an Elk Hair Caddis works nearly everywhere, but in clear, slow water use the CDC Caddis pattern. Egg-laying females can be imitated with a Soft Hackle or a Diving Caddis. In addition, the larval forms of the green rock worms and spotted caddis have specific imitations.

Caddis pupa

Caddis larva patterns should be dead-drifted on the river bottom. Pupa patterns can be dead-drifted on the bottom or just subsurface. In my experience, a Sparkle Pupa works well fished deep, but I prefer a Soft Hackle presented down-and-across for subsurface fishing. (There are anglers who disagree with me on this; we both catch fish.)

Adult caddis are presented like a normal dry fly. A fully-hackled Elk Hair Caddis is dandy for rough water, but you should trim the hackle off the bottom (nearly flush with the dubbing) when on a less bumpy stretch of river. And in quiet, clear water, a subtler pattern, such as the CDC Caddis, is best.

When imitating egg-layers, use a floating line and either dead-drift the fly near bottom or cast down-and-across and present the fly near the surface on a wet-fly swing.

Here are the main types of caddis you will encounter on Oregon rivers.

Green Rock Worm or Green Caddis (Rhyacophila). This is a free-living caddis (doesn't build a case). As you might expect from the name, larvae are green and worm-like. The larvae favor riffles, and they often drift in the current—and are often swallowed by trout. A larva pattern is effective beginning about a month before the hatch. The adults hatch in the afternoon from late spring through August. Females lay eggs by swimming or crawling into the water.

Spotted Caddis (Hydropsyche). This is another case-less caddis. Larvae are available to trout for much of the year. Many species are pale green and look a lot like the green rock worm, and are often found in the same kind of water. Net-spinning caddis live off drifting plankton, which they capture by building little nets in the crevices of rocks. Adults typically hatch from May through July.

Spotted caddis larva

Weedy-Water Caddis (Amiocentrus). A smallish caddis, the weedy-water caddis builds a round-shaped case. Hatches are April through June when most anglers are thinking about stoneflies. Trout, however, love these guys and will willingly switch to them when a hatch or egg-laying starts. Pupae, adults, and egg-laying females are all important.

Grannom (Brachycentrus). Grannoms build square-shaped cases in riffly water. The larvae are of limited significance, but pupae, adults, and egg-laying females are important. There are two hatch seasons: April and May, and July and August.

Grannom larva in case

Saddle Case Caddis (Glossosoma). These little guys build a case from pebbles and attach it to a large rock. They are so firmly attached that they are rarely found drifting in the current. Pupae, adults, and egg-laying females, however, are often taken.

October Caddis (Dicosmoecus). This is the Great Pumpkin of Oregon rivers, a caddis that is almost as large as a golden stonefly. As the name suggests, it emerges in fall. The larvae build cases of small pebbles, and neither the larvae nor the pupa are often eaten by trout, but the adults can make a juicy morsel. Egg-laying females are not important to anglers.

Lake-Dwelling Caddisflies

Lake-dwelling caddis are case builders. The larvae are seldom significant, but pupae and adults are often taken by trout. The same fly patterns that work in rivers also work in lakes, but it helps to add long antennae to the Elk Hair Caddis.

A pupa pattern can be simply cast and slowly retrieved; use an intermediate line so the fly is subsurface. However, there are several other (generally better) presentations. One is to cast a lightly-weighted Soft Hackle and let it slowly sink. Don't touch it! Just let it settle for 10 or 20 seconds, then slowly draw it towards you until it is near the surface. Then let it settle again.

Another pupa presentation is to cast the fly on a short line and let it settle to near the bottom; then draw the fly steadily to the surface in a near-vertical retrieve. A third method is wind drifting in an unanchored boat or float tube. To do this, use an intermediate line and cast either perpendicular or at a 45-degree angle to the wind. Then just hang on. You'll drift downwind, towing the fly behind you. Eventually the fly will be straight upwind from you so it is trolling water that you've drifted over. When that happens, pick up and cast again.

Stoneflies

Salmonfly (Pteronarcys californica). The salmonfly is the adult version of the giant stonefly. Nymphs live in the river for up to three years. When mature, the nymphs crawl to shore, climb onto alder trunks, grass stems, exposed rocks, and other out-of-the-water objects. The winged adult then emerges. And what a bug it is! At two-and-a-half inches long, with two pairs of wings and an orange body, it's hard to miss an adult salmonfly.

For three weeks, the adults crawl around on streamside vegetation in

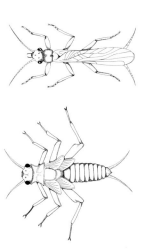

Stonefly adult (top) and nymph

search of a mate. Females then fly over the water, plop on the surface, and deposit their eggs. Or get sucked down by big trout.

Most of the salmonfly action happens near shore, first because the wind often blows them off overhanging alder branches or grass stems (or they simply fall off; they're really clumsy), and second because the egg-laying females usually stick close to land. Since adults are more active in warmer temperatures, most activity is in afternoon (wind-blown bugs) and at dusk (egg-laying).

The salmonfly hatch starts in mid-May and continues through mid-June. Adults are not the only action, however. For several weeks prior to the hatch season, nymphs often lose their grip on the bottom and are taken by waiting trout. Since prime stonefly habitat is in boulder fields and riffles, trout expect to see drifting nymphs in boulder fields and in deeper water just below riffles. Nymphs are taken all year long, but spring and fall are the best times.

Water temperature plays a key role in the salmonfly hatch. Hatches often start in the downstream sections of rivers where the water has had more time to warm up. Then the hatch works its way upstream.

After the hatch, there are still nymphs in the river, and trout will switch back to them in earnest in the fall. Some anglers use a smaller fly in fall, on the theory that the biggest nymphs hatched in spring. It sounds good, but I've never noticed that the trout cared one way or the other.

Golden Stonflies (Hesperoperla, Calineuria). Golden stones behave in a manner similar to salmonflies, but they are a tad smaller and begin hatching about two weeks later. Their hatch season overlaps with the salmonflies, so adults of both species are often available at the same time. I believe that given a choice, trout prefer the golden stones.

Little Yellow Stoneflies (Isoperla). Some rivers have significant populations of little yellow stoneflies. Nymphs are useful during the hatch season (but not very productive at other times). Adult imitations are fished in a manner similar to the larger stoneflies discussed above. While most little yellow stonefly adults hatch out on land, there is a species that emerges in the water like a mayfly.

Black Stoneflies (Capniidae). An often overlooked winter hatch, these small stoneflies are often taken by trout January through March. A size 16 or 18 black Elk Hair Caddis makes a good imitation.

Midges

There are so many midge species that it would be irrational to try to catalog them, so I'll just make a few general statements about them.

Midge pupa

The two-winged insects of the family Chironomidae are often called "chironomids" or "midges." There are river-dwelling and lake-dwelling species, but their emergence is similar: the larva (which is worm-like) changes into a pupa, and the mature pupa rises to the water's surface. Since midges are usually very small, the surface tension is a barrier to the pupae, and they hang suspended right at the surface. That is where trout most often take them: as a pupa just below the surface. If not eaten by a trout, the back of the pupa eventually pushes through the surface, and the adult emerges and quickly flies off.

In rivers, most midge action occurs in backeddies, occasionally in slow, flat runs, and sometimes even in fast water.

Adults form mating swarms, and midges locked in amorous embrace often fall back to the water. Trout are not romantics and will eat these mating clusters, so a dry fly such as the Griffiths Gnat or even a very small Elk Hair Caddis will sometimes take trout.

Midge hatches can be tricky to match. Because so many insects hatch at one time, trout become very selective, and you need to carefully match the size, color, and appearance of the natural insect. Because there are so many species, this can be difficult. When fishing in a river, seine the current (see below). Examine the seine for pupae, emerging adults, and shucks of the natural insect; match the size and color. In lakes, you can often find shucks and hatching midges on the surface. Again, examine carefully and match the size and color.

Dragonflies

Dragonfly nymphs are quite large and live in lakes, ponds, and very slow portions of rivers. Nymphs live several years, swimming around and eating other insects. When mature, they migrate to rocks, standing snags, and other above-water objects. They crawl out of the water, and the adult emerges.

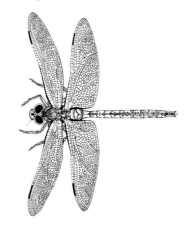
Adult dragonfly

Dragonfly adults are excellent fliers and are seldom taken by trout. The nymphs, however, are a large meal, and trout relish them.

Damselflies

Damselflies are closely related to dragonflies and have a similar life-cycle. However, damselflies are more numerous, and the nymphs are often eaten by fish. When mature, damselfly nymphs migrate in large numbers to above-water objects. This can provoke feeding frenzies by trout, who gorge themselves on the migrating nymphs.

Most hatches occur in July. After July there are few damselfly nymphs of any size to interest trout, so it is usually not productive to cast an imitation until the next spring. In August adult damsels are sometimes taken by trout.

Terrestrials

Terrestrials are insects that live on land. Gusts of wind, errors of navigation, and general bad luck sometimes conspire to drop terrestrials onto the water. For example, flying ants are commonly found on alpine lakes because the wind blows them out of nearby pine trees. Other terrestials that often become trout food are beetles and yellow jackets. If the spring months are dry, there will usually be a bumper crop of yellow jackets by late summer, and they can become important on both lakes and rivers.

Leeches

Leeches are worm-like creatures that live in still waters. Nearly every Oregon lake has leeches, but don't worry because they're not the blood-sucking kind. Most leeches that trout eat are between one and two inches long. Common colors are black, brown, gray-olive, and sometimes red.

Leeches swim with an up-and-down undulating motion, so fly patterns should be weighted more in the front half of the hook.

Most of their "swimming" is at night when it is illegal to fish for trout. However, fishing a leech pattern at dawn or dusk or on an overcast day can be quite productive.

Scuds

Scuds are a freshwater crustacean. They are related to shrimp, crabs, and crayfish. They live in shallow, weedy areas of lakes and slow portions of some rivers. They are light shy, so they're not out much except near dawn and dusk and on overcast days.

A swimming scud is straight, so pick an imitation tied on a straight hook when you are are going to retrieve a scud on a lake. Retrieve about eight inches of line, then pause a couple of seconds.

When drifting in a river, scuds curl up. So to imitate a drifting scud, use a fly tied on a curved hook, and dead drift it like it was a nymph.

Other Fish

Larger trout feed extensively on smaller fish, so if you want to catch old mossyback you'd do well to cast a good-sized fish pattern. The most common prey in Oregon lakes and rivers are tui chub (roach) and small whitefish. Zonkers are a decent imitation for both species. Sometimes a bit of yellow on the fly makes it more effective.

Finding Out What Lives in the Water

Always carry a seine so you can figure out what's going on with the bugs. Most fly shops sell some kind of commercial device, such as a fold-up kickscreen or a nymph net that covers a fishnet frame. At a minimum, find an old pair of nylon "footies" or the end of a nylon stocking. You can slip this over your hand like a mitt and use it to strain insects floating on the water.

The next step is to identify what you've found. The books mentioned at the beginning of this chapter will help you do that.

Hatch Chart

The next three pages summarize the aquatic insects of most interest to Oregon fly anglers. For each insect, I've shown the most important stages, the type of water that stage is found in, when that stage is an important trout food, and some suggestions for a fly pattern, including size and color choices. When an entry is "Same," it means "same as immediately above."

These charts should be regarded only as a starting point. Each river or lake may have its own timing for hatches, depending on the local environment, water temperature, etc. For example, October caddis are sometimes encountered on the Metolius River in May, but most of the rest of the state only sees that species in September and October.

Recipes for all the fly patterns listed in these charts can be found in this book. The suggested hook size is the Tiemco (TMC) hook appropriate for the fly pattern listed for each stage. Naturally, these are not the only fly patterns that will work. I have only listed ones that I know are effective and that are usually available at Oregon fly shops.

Mayflies

	Stage	Water Type	Season	Pattern	Size	Color
March Brown	Dun	Below riffles, flats	Mar-mid-April	Comparadun	12-14	Red-brown body, brown wing
	Dun*	Same	Same	Soft Hackle	12-14	Red-brown body
Green Drake	Nymph	Slow to moderate runs	Late May-mid-June	Poxyback Grn Drake	8-12	Olive body
	Dun	Same	Same	Paradrake Grn Drake	8-12	Olive body
Pale Morning Dun	Nymph	Slow to moderate runs, backeddies, bankside	June-July	Pheasant Tail, Hares Ear	16-18	Brown body
	Dun	Same	Same	Parachute PMD	16-18	Pale Yellow body, gray wing
	Spinner	Same	Same	CDC Spinner	18	Pale Yellow body, white wing
Yellow Quill	Dun*	Below riffles	June-July	Soft Hackle	12-14	Yellow body, tan or brown wing
Pale Evening Dun	Dun	Below riffles	May-July	Light Cahill	12-16	Yellow body, light tan wing
Trico	Dun	Slow runs, lakes	Aug, Sept	Trico Paradun	20-22	Dark body, light wing
	Spinner	Same	Same	CDC spinner	20-22	Dark body, white wing (male); Tan body, white wing (female)
Slate-Winged Olive	Nymph	Slow runs, flats	July, Aug	Poxyback Grn Drake	10-14	Olive body
	Dun	Same	Same	Paradrake Grn Drake	10-14	Olive body
Mahogany Dun	Nymph	Slow water	Sept-Oct	Pheas. Tail, Hares Ear	12-16	Red-brown body
	Dun	Same	Same	Comparadun	12-16	Red-brown body, gray wing
Blue-winged olive	Nymph	Flats, backeddies	Sept-April	Hares Ear, Pheasant Tail	16-20	Brown body
	Emerger	Same	Same	Floating nymph	16-20	Olive body
	Dun	Same	Same	Parachute *Baetis*	16-20	Olive body, gray wing
	Spinner	Same	Same	CDC Spinner	16-20	Olive body, white wing
Speckle-Winged Quill	Nymph	Lakes, very slow water	May-Sept	Flashback Phsnt Tail	14-18	Brown
	Dun	Same	Same	Adams, Comparadun	14-18	Gray body, gray wing
Hex	Nymph	Lakes, very slow water	early July	Burk's Hexagenia	4-8	Tan body
	Dun	Same	Same	Paradrake Hex	4-8	Yellow body

* Dun emerges underwater

Caddis

	Stage	Water Type	Season	Pattern	Size	Color
Green Rock Worm	Larva	Riffles, below riffles	Apr, May, Aug-Oct	Green Rock Worm	12-14	Green body, black head
	Pupa	Same	May, Sept-Oct	Sparkle Pupa, Sparkle Quill, Soft Hackle	12-14	Green body, tan shroud
	Adult	Bankside	Same	Elk Hair Caddis, CDC Caddis	14	Dark olive body, gray wing
	Egg-layer	Midriver	Same	Diving Caddis, Soft Hackle	14	Dark olive body, dark wing
Spotted Caddis	Larva	Riffles, below riffles	Jan-Aug, Nov, Dec	Randalls Caddis, Zug Bug	12	Green body
	Pupa	Same	Jun-Aug	Sparkle Pupa, Sparkle Quill, Soft Hackle	12-14	Olive body, tan shroud
	Adult	Bankside	Same	Elk Hair Caddis, CDC Caddis	14	Brown to tan body, tan wing
	Egg-layer	Midriver, riffles	Same	Diving Caddis, Soft Hackle	14	Brown body, dark wing
Saddle-Case Caddis	Pupa	Below riffles	April, Aug-Oct	Sparkle Pupa, Sparkle Quill, Soft Hackle	18-20	Yellow body, tan shroud
	Adult	Bankside	Same	Elk Hair Caddis, CDC Caddis	18-20	Tan body, dark wing
	Egg-layer	Riffles, runs	Same	Diving Caddis, Soft Hackle	18-20	Same
Grannom	Pupa	Below riffles	Apr, May	Sparkle Pupa, Sparkle Quill, Soft Hackle	14-16	Green body, tan shroud
	Adult	Bankside	Same	Elk Hair Caddis, CDC Caddis	14-16	Dark brown body, tan wing
	Egg-layer	Midriver, riffles	Same	Diving Caddis, Soft Hackle	14-16	Dark body, dark wing
Weedy-Water Caddis	Pupa	Moderate-slow runs	April-July	Sparkle Pupa, Sparkle Quill, Soft Hackle	16-18	Green body, tan shroud
	Adult	Bankside	Same	Elk Hair Caddis, CDC Caddis	16-18	Dark olive body, dark wing
	Egg-layer	Runs	Same	Diving Caddis, Soft Hackle	16-18	Dark body, dark wing
October Caddis	Adult	Bankside, seams	Sept, Oct	Stimulator	4	Orange body, tan wing

Other Hatches

	Stage	Water Type	Season	Pattern	Size	Color
Salmonfly	Nymph	Boulder fields, below riffles	April-June	Kaufmanns Stone, Rubber Legs	4-6	Black, brown
	Adult	Bankside	Mid-May -Jun	MacSalmon, Clarks Stonefly, Stimulator Madam X	6-10	Orange body, dark wing
Golden Stonefly	Nymph	Boulder fields, below riffles	April-June	Kaufmanns Stone, Rubber Legs	6-8	Mottled tan
	Adult	Bankside	Late May -Jun	MacSalmon, Stimulator	6-10	Gold-yellow body, light wing
Little Yellow Stonefly	Nymph	Riffles	July-Sept	Hares Ear	8-14	Mottled brown and tan
	Adult	Bankside	Same	Stimulator, Elk Hair Caddis	8-14	Yellow body, light wing
Winter Black Stonefly	Adult	Bankside, backeddies	Jan-Mar	Elk Hair Caddis	16-18	Black
Midge	Larva	Lakes	All year	Midge Pupa	16-20	Red body
	Pupa	Lakes, rivers	All year	Same	10-22	Black, gray, olive, red, or tan
	Adult	Lakes, slow water	All year	Griffiths Gnat	18	Peacock herl body
Dragonfly	Nymph	Lakes, very slow water	All year	Lake Dragon, Woolly Bugger	6-10	Olive or brown
Damselfly	Nymph	Lakes, very slow water	Apr -July	Marabou Damsel	8-10	Olive, yellow olive
	Adult	Same	Aug	Stalcup Damsel	8-10	Blue with black stripes or Dull green with black stripes

Flies for Trout

The fly recipes listed in this book are effective, proven patterns that are available at most Oregon fly shops. The hook models and sizes are for Tiemco hooks, which are also widely available. Other manufacturers often have similar hooks, but the industry lacks standardization, so if you use a different hook such as Mustad, make sure you make an adjustment in size or you will end up with a fly that isn't quite right.

I have used fly recipes from a series of books by Randall Kaufmann: *Tying Nymphs, Tying Dry Flies,* and *Fly Patterns of Umpqua Feather Merchants.* The first two books have step-by-step instructions and photos showing how to construct many of these flies. Randall is an Oregon fly tyer and fly designer of national reputation.

You'll find below an index of patterns described in other chapters of this book. This is followed by recipes for more flies.

Trout Fly Patterns Listed in Earlier Chapters

Nymphs, Larvae, and Pupae

Pheasant Tail Nymph/Flashback Pheasant Tail
(Original by Frank Sawyer)

Hook:	3761, sizes 10-18
Thread:	To match pheasant tail
Tail:	Pheasant tail fibers to match abdomen
Rib:	Copper wire
Abdomen:	Pheasant tail, olive or brown; wrap forward
Wingcase:	Pheasant tail to match abdomen
Thorax:	Peacock herl
Legs:	Pheasant tail to match abdomen
Head:	Copper wire

This can be tied unweighted, or weighted with lead on the shank or with a bead head. The Flashback Pheasant Tail has a strip of pearl Flashabou down the back and uses Flashabou for the wingcase.

Poxyback Green Drake
(Mike Mercer)

Hook:	200R, sizes 10-12
Thread:	Olive
Tail:	Three grouse or hen saddle fibers
Back:	Dark golden brown turkey
Gills:	One or two olive filoplumes
Rib:	Copper Wire
Abdomen:	Dark brown-olive Antron
Wingcase:	Dark turkey
Legs:	Grouse tied flat over thorax
Thorax:	Same as abdomen. Pick out dubbing so it's fuzzy
Head:	Same as body

When fly is completed, put one drop of 5-minute expoxy on top of the wingcase and let it dry while the fly is upright. When a nymph is mature and the dun is moments from emerging, the wingcase often englarges and develops a shine. The epoxy on this fly imitates that feature. Similar ties can be developed for other mayfly species.

Burk's Hexagenia
(Andy Burk)

Hook: 200R, sizes 4-8

Thread: Primrose or pale yellow

Tail: Gray marabou

Back: Turkey quill

Gills: Gray pheasant filoplume tied on top of hook (not wrapped)

Rib: Copper wire

Abdomen: Pale yellow rabbit

Wingcase: Turkey tail

Thorax: Same as abdomen

Legs: Mottled hen saddle

One of the keys to this fly's effectiveness is the filoplume pheasant "gills." Form the abdomen first, then pull the filoplume over the top of it. The fly should be weighted and fished near the bottom with a lift-and-settle retrieve beginning a few hours before the hatch.

Green Rock Worm
(Randall Kaufmann variant of Polly Rosborough pattern)

Hook: 200R or 2457, sizes 12-18; weighted

Thread: Black

Rib: Green wire

Abdomen: Cream-green Antron (caddis blend 5)

Head: Black Haretron blended with abdomen material (keep small)

Zug Bug
(Cliff Zug)

Hook: 5262 or 3761, sizes 10-14; weighted

Thread: Black

Tail: 5-8 fibers of peacock sword

Rib: Silver tinsel

Abdomen: Peacock herl

Legs: Brown or furnace hackle, beard-style

Wingcase: Mallard dyed woodduck

Rubber Leqgs

Hook: 5263, sizes 2-8; heavily weighted

Thread: Black

Antennae: Black rubber

Tail: Black rubber

Body: Black chenille

I use four strips of rubber, two on each side. They're arranged so each strip makes one leg and one antenna or tail. That only makes four legs, where a real insect would have six, but I use this fly in fast water where trout don't have enough time to count.

Serendipity
(Mike Lawson)

Hook: 2457, sizes 14-20

Thread: Red

Abdomen: Two strands of red Z-lon or Antron yarn, twisted and wrapped tightly. Wrap front to back, then reverse and overwrap back to front.

Rib: Silver tinsel (optional)

Head: Natural caribou or deer body hair. Secure on top of hook, then trim close in front, a bit longer in back.

In this dressing and on a size 18 hook, the Serendipity makes a good blood midge imitation. It can also be tied in black, olive, brown, tan.

Lake Dragon
(Randall Kaufmann)

Hook: 5263, sizes 6-10; weighted, with lead flattened in rear half

Thread: To match abdomen

Eyes: Burned monofilament

Tail: Marabou to match abdomen

Rib: Copper wire

Abdomen: Olive or brown Haretron blended with goat hair of different hues

Legs: Pheasant body fibers to match abdomen

Wingcase: Turkey; use a Pantone pen to color

Head: Same as abdomen

Floating Nymph
(Mike Lawson)

Hook: 900BL, sizes 16-18

Thread: Brown

Tail: A few blue dun hackle fibers

Abdomen: Superfine, yellow-tan
Wing: Ball of light gray poly dubbing
Thorax: Same as abdomen
Legs: Same as tail

This dressing is for an emerging pale morning dun. Tied on a size 18 or 20 hook and with olive dubbing and thread, it would represent a blue-winged olive.

Sparkle Pupa
(Gary LaFontaine)
Hook: 900BL, sizes 12-20
Thread: Brown
Shroud: Tan Antron "ballooned" over abdomen. Leave a few fibers trailing out the back
Abdomen: Green Antron
Wing: Light deer hair tied sparse
Head: Dark brown Haretron or marabou

A traditional tie that is available at most shops. Vary the body and wing colors to match the natural insects (see the hatch chart).

Sparkle Quill
(Mike Mercer)
Hook: 2457, sizes 12-18
Thread: Flourescent green
Shroud: Tan Z-lon sparsely tied over the top half of the fly
Abdomen: Thin flouscent green Antron
Rib: Bright green turkey biot
Legs: Brown partridge fibers tied beard style and as long as the abdomen
Wings: Light dun Z-lon tied in sparse clump
Antennae: Woodduck or mallard dyed woodduck, trailing over back
Head: Light olive or gray-brown olive marabou, twisted and wrapped

A better pupa pattern, but less widely available. Vary the body and shroud colors to match the natural insects (see the hatch chart).

Soft Hackle/Hares Ear Soft Hackle
Hook: 5262, 3761, 900BL, or 200R; sizes 10-18
Thread: To match body
Abdomen: Floss

Thorax: Hares ear
Legs: Gray or brown partridge tied so fibers extend past hook point

Soft Hackles are dynamite in caddis-rich rivers because they can look like either a caddis pupa or an egg-laying female. They are also extremely easy to tie. Vary the body and wing colors to match the natural insects (see the hatch chart).

To tie a Hares Ear Soft Hackle, skip the thorax and use Haretron dubbing for the body. Weighting with a few turns of very thin lead will help it break through the surface tension.

Diving Caddis
(Gary LaFontaine)
Hook: 9300, sizes 14-18
Thread: Black
Body: Antron
Underwing: Partridge
Overwing: Clear Antron

Vary the body and wing colors to match the natural insects (see hatch chart). Caddis turn darker as they get ready to lay eggs. Tie this pattern sparse.

Dry Flies

No Hackle PMD
(Doug Swisher and Carl Richards)
Hook: 900BL, sizes 16-18
Thread: Yellow
Tail: Blue dun hackle fibers, split
Body: Pale yellow Superfine
Wing: Gray duck quill

When wild rainbows are rising to a PMD hatch on a slow, clear spring creek, a downstream presentation of a No Hackle fly may be the only tactic that will produce trout. One problem: after two or three hookups the wing is shredded and the fly is history.

Comparadun, March Brown
(Al Caucci and Bob Nastasi)
Hook: 900BL, size 12-16
Thread: Brown
Wing: Mottled brown deer hair tied upright and flared

Tail: Blue dun hackle fibers, split

Body: Red-brown Superfine

The comparadun style rides well and floats without hackle, which is an advantage on slow, quiet stretches. The fly is more durable than a No Hackle, but not quite as effective. On a size 18 hook with a pale yellow body, it makes a good PMD pattern. Other insects can be imitated by varying the body and wing colors.

Light Cahill
(Dan Cahill)

Hook: 900BL, sizes 12-20

Thread: Pale Yellow

Wing: Mallard flank dyed wooduck, tied upright and divided in traditional Catskill dry fly fashion

Tail: Hackle fibers to match body

Body: Ginger or cream Superfine

Hackle: To match body

This pattern has been around over 100 years, and it's still catching trout.

Trico Parachute Dun

Hook: 900BL, sizes 18-22

Thread: Black

Tail: White hackle fibers, split

Wing: White hen hackle tip

Body Black Superfine

Hackle: Grizzly hackle, parachute style

Cripple
(Bob Quigley)

Hook: 900BL, sizes 14-18

Thread: To match body

Shuck: Tan Z-lon over marabou or hackle fibers

Rib: Copper wire

Body: Pheasant tail or Haretron

Thorax: Superfine

Wing: Natural deer, clipped short in back and left long in front

Hackle: Grizzly

During a mayfly hatch, a small percentage of duns never make it out of the nymph shuck. Trout have a hard time resisting a cripple because they know it won't get away from them; a cripple is "easy pickin's." Vary the body and thorax colors to match a PMD, *Callibaetis*, blue-winged olive, etc.

CDC Spinner
(House of Harrop)

Hook: 900BL, sizes 12-20

Thread: To match body

Tail: Blue dun hackle fibers, split

Body: Superfine; see below

Wing: Blue dun CDC

Thorax: Superfine to match body

This is a general recipe. For a PMD spinner, use pale yellow body dubbing on a size 18 hook; for a blue-winged olive spinner, use dark olive and size16-20 hooks; for a Callibaetis spinner, use tan dubbing on size 14-18 hooks.

CDC Caddis
(House of Harrop)

Hook: 900BL, sizes 12-20

Thread: To match body

Abdomen: Antron

Underwing: Z-lon, color to match abdomen

Overwing: CDC feather

Thorax: Same as abdomen

Legs: Butt ends of overwing extend at a right angle from thorax

Abodmen and wing colors to match natural insects (see chart)

X Caddis
(Craig Mathews and John Juracek)

Hook: 900BL, sizes 12-20

Thread: To match body

Shroud: Gold Z-lon trailing behind fly

Body: Antron

Wing: Deer hair, tied similar to Elk Hair Caddis

This is a good imitation of a crippled caddis (one that got stuck coming out of the pupal shroud). Vary abodmen and wing colors to match natural insects (see chart)

Griffiths Gnat
(George Griffith)

Hook: 900BL, sizes 18-22

Thread: Black

Rib: Fine copper wire

Body: Peacock herl

Hackle: Grizzly, palmered

Yellow Jacket
(Andy Burk)

Hook: 5263, size 10

Thread: Black

Eyes: Extra small monofilament nymph eyes

Body: Alternating bands of yellow and black Antron

Wings: Furnace hackle tips, swept-wing style

Head: Black Antron

Legs: Brown hackle

four feathers laid vertically along the back. Clip the underside before tying so you get a better fit. Wing is twice hook length

Hackle: Grizzly to match body color

Muddler
(Don Gapen)

Hook: 5263, sizes 2-12; weight is optional

Thread: Black

Tail: Turky quill

Body: Gold Diamond Braid (or gold tinsel)

Underwing: Gray squirrel tail

Wing: Turkey quill

Collar: Spun natural deer hair

Head: Caribou or deer hair, spun and clipped

Baitfish

Zonker

Hook: 5263, sizes 2-8; weighted

Thread: White

Body: Mylar piping tied front and back and shaped to look like a fish body

Wing: Rabbit strip. Tie at front and back, then fix with cement or Pliobond. Let rabbit strip trail out the back as long as the hook shank.

Throat: Rabbit

Eyes: Painted eyes (optional)

Zonkers are good baitfish patterns. Tie in these combinations: silver body/white wing; copper body/ gray wing; olive body/olive wing.

Matuka

Hook: 5263, sizes 2-8; weight is optional

Thread: To match body

Rib: Copper wire

Body: Chenille (olive, brown, or black)

Gills: Red yarn or dubbing

Wing: Hen hackle to match body. Use

Guides

Some reasons to hire a professional fishing guide are: they fish the same areas day-in and day-out, so they know what works best under all conditions; they can help you improve your fishing skills; they know the unobvious places to find fish, especially when it's crowded; they have the skills and equipment to get you safely down a whitewater river; they can loan or rent to you equipment you don't have; and you get to relax and concentrate on having a good time. Even expert fly anglers often hire a guide when fishing a new river or lake. It's an investment in better fishing.

A typical price for a one-day outing is $300-$400 for two anglers. It is customary to tip a guide, especially if you've had a good time. A typical tip is $20 per angler.

Most guides are amiable, skilled people who want you to have a good time. Unfortunately there are a few folks who call themselves guides, but who really ought to be in another business. How do you ensure that you get a good guide? First, ask your friends and acquaintances if they have used a fishing guide and what their experience was like. Next, make sure you choose a guide who is familiar with the water you are going to fish; ask a prospective guide how long he has been guiding the water you are going to. Also, ask what percentage of the guide's trips are fly fishing.

Some fly shops have their own guide service, while others can recommend a competent guide. The Oregon Outdoor Association is another source . Their members are professional outdoor guides and outfitters, most of whom do it full time. To get a brochure listing their guides, call 800/747-9552.

To get the most out of a guided trip, make sure you and the guide understand what each of you wants and has to offer. Be frank and objective about your skills; if you are a beginner, make sure the guide understands that. If you want lots of fish, but don't care about the size, tell the guide. If you want trophies, but will settle for fewer hookups, make sure the guide knows. If you have spe-cial diet requirements, tell your guide before he packs a lunch. Health concerns or handicaps? Let your guide know! Fishing tactics you "don't do"? Tell the guide. Want to take home lots of fish in a cooler? Say so before you hire your guide, because most fly fishing guides advocate catch-and-release. How long do you want to fish? All day for some folks is eight hours, but for others it's dawn to dusk. Should you bring your own lunch and water? What about snacks or alcohol? Make sure these questions are answered *before* the day of the trip. And when the guide tells you to meet at a certain time, *be prompt!*

If your casting skills are rusty, take a fly casting lesson from a local fly shop; a $30 investment in a lesson can help you get the most out of your $300 trip.

Here are some guides I've fished with and feel confident in listing. See the next chapter for the phone numbers of fly shops.

Mark Bachman. Deschutes trout and steelhead, Sandy River steelhead; The Fly Fishing Shop, Welches.

Sterling Becklin (Silversides Guide Service). Rogue steelhead. 541/474-2871.

Jim Dexter. Crane Prairie, Davis Lake, East Lake; Deschutes River Outfitters, Bend.

Fred Foisett. Crane Prairie, Davis Lake, East Lake, Deschutes River; The Hook, Sunriver.

Gavin Grant. Williamson trout; Williamson River Anglers, Chiloquin.

Rick Killingsworth (High Desert Drifters). Deschutes trout and steelhead. 541/389-0607.

Gary Krauss. Rogue steelhead, Williamson and Wood trout. 541/597-4330.

Bill Kremers. Deschutes trout and steelhead. 541/754-6411.

Mike McLucas. Deschutes trout and steelhead. 541/395-2611.

Denny Rickards. Upper Klamath Lake. 541/381-2218.

John Smeraglio. Deschutes trout and steelhead; Deschutes Canyon Fly Shop.

Mike St. John. Rogue steelhead; McKenzie Outfitters, Medford.

Oregon Fly Shops

Ashland

Ashland Outdoor Store
37 Third St.
Ashland, OR 97520
541/488-1202

Astoria

Salmon Republic
3292 Leif Erikson Dr., Lower Level
Astoria, OR 97103
503/325-7587

Bend/Sunriver

Deschutes River Outfitters
61115 S. Hwy 97
Bend, OR 97702
541/388-8191

The Fly Box
1293 NE 3rd St.
Bend, OR 97701
541/388-3330

The Hook
Bldg 21 Sunriver Mall
Sunriver, OR 97707
541/593-2358

The Patient Angler
55 NW Wall St.
Bend, OR 97701
541/389-6208

Sunriver Fly Shop
#1 Venture Lane, Sunriver Business Park
Sunriver, OR 97707
541/593-8814

Chiloquin/Klamath Falls

Williamson River Anglers
Junction of Hwys 97 and 62
Chiloquin, OR 97624
541/783-2677

Enterprise/Joseph

Joseph Fly Shoppe
203 N. Main
Joseph, OR 97846
541/432-4343

Eugene/Corvallis

The Caddis Fly168 W. 6th Ave.
Eugene, OR 97401
541/342-7005

Homewaters
444 W. 3rd Ave.
Eugene, OR 97401
541/342-6691

The Scarlet Ibis
905 NW Kings Bvd
Corvallis, OR 97330
541/754-1544

Hood River

Gorge Fly Shop
201 Oak St
Hood River, OR 97031
541/386-6977

La Grande

Four Seasons Fly Shop
10210 Wallowa Lake Hwy
La Grande, OR 97850
541/963-8420

Maupin

Deschutes Canyon Fly Shop
599 S. Hwy 97
Maupin, OR 97037
541/395-2565

Medford

McKenzie Outfitters
1340 Biddle Rd
Medford, OR 97504
541/773-5145

Portland Area

Countrysport
1201 SW Morrison Ave.
Portland, OR 97205
503/221-4545

Fisherman's Marine Supply
1120 N. Hayden Meadows Dr.
Portland, OR 97217
503/282-0044

Fisherman's Marine Supply
Oregon City Shopping Center
1900 SE McLoughlin #60
Oregon City, OR 97545
503/557-3313

Kaufmann's Streamborn
8861 SW Commercial
Tigard, OR 97223
503/639-6400

NW Flyfishing Outfitters
17302 NE Halsey St.
Gresham, OR 97230
503/252-1529
888-292-1137

Prineville

Fin N Feather Fly Shop
785 W 3rd
Prineville, OR 97754
541/447-8691

Roseburg Area

Blue Heron
109 Hargis Ln.
Idleyld, OR 97447
541/496-0448

Salem

Creekside Fly Shop
345 High St. SE
Salem, OR 97301
503/588-1768

Fly Country Outfitters
3400 State St., Suite G704
Salem, OR 97
503/585-4898
www.flycountry.com

Valley Fly Fisher
153 Alice Ave. S.
Salem, OR 97302
503/375-3721

Sisters

The Fly Fishers Place
151 W. Main
Sisters, OR 97759
541/549-3474

Welches

The Fly FIshing Shop
Hoodland Park Plaza
68248 E. Hwy 26
Welches, OR 97067
503/622-4607

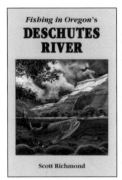